I BELIEVE IN HEAVEN ON EARTH

I Believe in

Heaven on Earth

Life after life for humanity
and planet Earth

Tony and Patricia Higton

Hodder & Stoughton
LONDON SYDNEY AUCKLAND

Typeset by Avon Dataset Ltd, Bidford-on-Avon, Warks

Printed and bound in Great Britain by
The Guernsey Press Co. Ltd, Channel Isles

Hodder & Stoughton
A Division of Hodder Headline Ltd
338 Euston Road
London NW1 3BH

This book is dedicated
to Michel
with gratitude
for advice and encouragement

Contents

Editor's Preface

This new series is intended to build on the widely-acknowledged success of the original 'I Believe' series, of which several volumes continue to be in print. Now as then, each book sets out to tackle one of the key issues which faces Christians today. The overall aim is to stimulate informed thinking and to encourage living faith by building a bridge between the ever-relevant teaching of the Bible and the complex realities of the modern world.

At the dawn of a new millennium, there is a growing and urgent interest in what the Bible says about the future. How near is the end of life as we know it? What can we expect to happen? What steps can we take to get ready?

The problem is that, for most people, what the Bible says about these questions seems to be an inpenetrable maze. There are so many complex and contradictory interpretations on offer that many of us prefer to bypass the subject altogether. Preachers too are wary of diving into the murky waters of the Last Things in case they get out of their depth and end up more confused than they were to start with!

It's perhaps characteristic of the Higtons that, when I first approached Tony about writing for this series, this was the subject at the top of his list. He and Patricia have never been afraid to tackle controversial issues head-on and this book is further evidence of their passionate commitment to help Christians know and live by the teaching of the Bible in every area of life.

I'm grateful to them for what they have written and anticipate that it will be a stimulating and thought-provoking eye-opener for many people. You may not agree with everything Tony and Patricia say in this book – but it will certainly challenge you to work out more precisely what you *do* believe and why you believe it in this vital area of Christian thought and action.

David Stone

Foreword

The turn of a millennium invites us to look forward – forward not only to the morning after the party, but to God's ultimate intention for us and for the world. Only by understanding that can we hope to make sense of our lives today. Tony and Patricia Higton offer a biblical answer to big questions:

Is there life after death?
What is the future of the world?
What does it mean to affirm that Jesus will come again?
Is hell out of date?
How do we unravel biblical prophecy?
How does hope based on Jesus Christ change the way we live?

I welcome their forthright book for several reasons: it discusses differing views with courtesy; it looks for the middle ground wherever possible; it emphasises that Christian hope is focused on Christ himself, not merely on the 'end of the world'; it sets out clearly what it means to live as people who are grasped by hope. Tired of millennium hype? Try Christian hope!

Dr Stephen H. Travis MA PhD
Vice Principal, St John's Nottingham

Introduction

The future of planet Earth; questions about heaven; annihilation or hell; the return of Christ; a special Millennium; fulfilled and future prophecies; the destiny of Israel; the meaning of the book of Revelation; and whether being more informed about these issues helps in this life – what does the world's best-seller have to say on these topics?

If the average person in the street, the person in the pew or a church leader wants to know what is taught in the Bible about all things future, the choice of books seems to be mainly between sensational fundamentalist publications or abstruse academic works. There are a few books in between, most of which either stress a particular view or seem to be concerned to play down any drama, emphasising rather such concepts as hope. Important though that is, it is a pity if the drama which undoubtedly characterises the biblical teaching is watered down – after all, the end of everything as we know it cannot fail to be cataclysmic!

We shall confront such matters head-on, aiming to open up these mind-blowing subjects in a way which may interest both the agnostic and the committed Christian (who may have little understanding of such matters, or be fairly knowledgeable but open to fresh insights). We hope too that this book will be useful not only to individuals, but for group discussion, for example in church homegroups, perhaps for a new millennium study course.

We also aim to interest and inform those who have previously avoided teaching these issues because they have been bedevilled by controversy. It is our conviction that it is not only possible, but vital, for Christians to be in agreement on primary issues related to 'the Last Things', while agreeing to disagree over secondary matters. We ourselves used to hold a particular view of the Millennium, etc., which we taught in conferences on the subject. We have since learned greater humility when tackling such daunting issues. Naturally we convey our creative ideas with passion but, we trust, without dogmatism. It is our fervent hope that many with a teaching ministry in the Church will discover a renewed confidence to convey these vital subjects.

In the first few chapters, we have kept quotations and references to a minimum, and where they are more necessary, in the second half of the book, we have included most of them in the text so that the reader will not be distracted by having to look them up. This will particularly help those unfamiliar with the Bible. In the hope that we shall publish a more academic book on these subjects in the future, with an extensive bibliography, we have not attempted to include one for this book.

Many people are so earthly minded they are no heavenly use. While hoping to stir folk out of that mind-set, we do not want to encourage the opposite mentality. We shall endeavour to show how even basic understanding of these issues should transform our lives here and now. It is equally important to be reminded that, whether or not any of us is alive on the earth when the bigger picture unfolds, each one of us will have to face our own 'end time'. This book deals not only with the future of planet Earth, but with what lies in store for every human being.

Patricia and Tony Higton

Chapter 1

What on earth will happen?

'The heavens will disappear with a roar; the elements will be destroyed by fire, and the earth and everything in it will be laid bare.'

(2 Pet. 3:10)

An endangered planet

Will the human race, or even planet Earth, survive for another thousand years? This is the question-mark which looms large over the dawn of the twenty-first century. Although people consult prophets of all kinds, whether scientists or mystics, relatively few take the trouble to try to understand the teaching of the Bible on the subject. Yet it encompasses the entire sweep of the human story, from before the beginning to beyond the end of time. From it we may learn so much about the future of individuals, humanity and even the earth. In fact, the Bible is the greatest prophetic book of all time. The vivid picture of the future painted there is one of stark contrast: between light, peace, the wonder of eternal life with God; and darkness, despair, even destruction.

Our world is also one of contrasting scenarios. It was only twenty years after scientists had provided the human race with the capability of blowing the earth to smithereens that human beings saw from a new perspective just how much we had to lose. Satellites presented us in the 1960s with the first ever images taken from space of our planet. Now at last we could see our globe in its totality, seemingly so fragile, breathtaking in its beauty, the sight of it capable of inspiring a response of awe, poetic description and even religious conversion on the part of many astronauts. One of them, Pham Tuam of Vietnam, wrote:

> I have been in love with the sky since birth. And when I could fly, I wanted to go higher, to enter space and become a 'man of the heights'. During the eight days I spent in space, I realised that mankind needs heights to better know our long-suffering Earth, to see what cannot be seen close up. Not just to love her beauty, but also to ensure that we do not bring even the slightest harm to the natural world. (*The Home Planet* edited by Kevin W. Kelley, Addison-Wesley 1988, p. 85)

During the decades which followed, human beings came to understand much more about the intricacy and interconnected-ness of life on earth. We began to realise that, from the industrial revolution onwards, we have unwittingly been upsetting that delicate balance, and it is proving well-nigh impossible to reverse the damage done. One scenario is of global warming which could change life as we know it for thousands of years to come, but some dismiss or ignore the warnings of those who campaign with such vigour to sound the alarm. While many try to save our planet, others continue to place its entire future at risk. Leaders of responsible governments, fully informed of the enormous dangers atomic weapons pose to the human race, assure us they are concerned only to keep the minimum nuclear arsenal necessary to maintain world peace. But there are others, whether power-hungry dictators or terrorists, who constitute a far greater threat. The situation has been even more precarious since the Iron Curtain collapsed, the breakdown of Communism resulting in loss of control over the vast military network which had been so carefully organised for decades. We get so used to living on top of such a powder keg that it is easy to forget that it was only well into the twentieth century that, for the first time ever, humanity developed the lethal capability of destroying most of life as we know it. Apparently, as recently as 1995, Russia only aborted a ten-minute countdown to a retaliatory ballistic missile launch when it was realised, after five minutes, that the supposed approach of an American Trident missile was in fact a Norwegian weather research rocket. Colonel Bykov, former commander of a mobile Russian missile regiment, commented on the Channel 4 *Equinox* 'Russian Roulette' programme in July 1998 that this was due to the poor state of their early warning systems.

It is common knowledge that enough atomic bombs exist to destroy civilisation many times over, but biological and chemical weapons are also stockpiled. On 26 November 1997 one such horror was reported in *The Times*:

> The United Nations believes that Saddam Hussein may have produced enough of the deadly VX chemical weapon to kill everyone on Earth, William Cohen, the US Defense Secretary, said yesterday. 'Originally, the Iraqis indicated they had just a small quantity of VX. One drop on your finger will produce death in a matter of a few moments. Now, the UN believes that Saddam may have produced as much as 200 tons. And this, theoretically, would be enough to kill every man, woman and child on the face of the Earth.'

Certain natural phenomena also pose a threat to life on earth. Geologists have long known about cycles of Ice Ages, which of course have devastating implications for plant and animal life. More recently, research has shown that comets and asteroids have struck before and could do so again. The last asteroid to make a major impact destroyed 900 square miles of forest in Siberia on 30 June 1908. It has been calculated that this rogue hunk of rock from the asteroid belt, which circles the sun between Mars and Jupiter, approached the earth at 50,000 m.p.h., exploding like a fifteen-megaton bomb above ground. If a major city had been below, it would have been totally destroyed by this missile, one thousand times more powerful than the Hiroshima bomb. There is a strong body of opinion which attributes the demise of the dinosaurs to the after-effects of a far bigger asteroid impact in what is now the Gulf of Mexico. It is interesting that 'catastrophism', once dismissed as alarmist, is now in vogue with both geologists and cosmologists, as a term to describe past and possible future devastation of life on this planet. Some assess that at least four major cataclysmic events have overwhelmed the earth, totally redirecting its formation and life. (But at least we may console ourselves with the knowledge that catastrophe led ultimately to renewal of life.) At the time of writing, it has been revealed that a far bigger asteroid than the one which devastated a Siberian forest will pass 'close' to the earth on 26 October 2028. Initial calculations estimated that it might pass earth at a distance of 30,000 miles – eight times closer than the moon – but the calculations, we were informed, could be inaccurate either way. At one stage, astronomers were warning that they could not rule out a direct hit. An impact on land would create a blast equivalent to two million Hiroshima-sized bombs, resulting in incalculable effects. Dr Daniel Green, of the Harvard–Smithsonian Center for Astrophysics in Cambridge, Massachusetts, commented: 'It would be disastrous, and it would have significance globally.' Subsequent calculations found that this 'Doomsday Asteroid' would pass earth considerably further away than the original estimation.

It was sobering to hear a news bulletin, in December 1997, reporting that a meteorite of between fifty and one hundred metres across had just been seen over Greenland, travelling at such speed that when it struck, it disappeared for ever, buried deep beneath the snow and ice. A few years previously huge excitement was engendered among astronomers when the comet Shoemaker–Levy 9 struck Jupiter in July 1994. Never before in the history of recorded astronomy had the collision between two bodies in the solar system been observed. Every observatory in the world turned to look at this awesome event, which in fact exceeded all expectations. There was a flash in the atmosphere, mind-blowing in its enormity, followed by the resulting twenty huge 'fragments' of the comet exploding as they impacted Jupiter, releasing more energy than all the nuclear weapons ever made. Fragment G was the biggest, its demise creating an atmospheric feature which computerised pictures show to be at least twice the size of earth. Writing in the magazine *Astronomy Now* in

January 1995, Jacqueline Mitton pointed out that the comet not only scarred the planet, but

> struck directly at a complacent view held by many people of a safe, benign Solar System where dangerous impacts ceased billions of years ago . . . We observed from a safe distance . . . But, psychologically, the comet hit close to home. For the Solar System astronomers who have been agitating for years about the risk to Earth posed by errant rocks in space, the warning could hardly have been better timed. Suddenly they had to be taken seriously.

The dramatic language of the Bible used to be dismissed as exaggeration – but what could be more dramatic than some discoveries of modern scientific research? It was fascinating to note that one television programme on asteroids and comets (icy bodies from the outer solar system) actually began with a quotation from the book of Revelation: 'a great star, blazing like a torch, fell from the sky on a third of the rivers and on the springs of water . . . A third of the waters turned bitter, and many people died' (Rev. 8:10–11). The opening words of the documentary were: 'For centuries the Scriptures have pictured the end of the world coming in a gigantic fire-ball from the sky. But astronomers now realise there are good scientific reasons for such ideas.'

Once upon a time

When faced with the possibility of such devastation, we human beings realise how much we love our planet, our solar system and, indeed, the universe. The night sky, when not dimmed for observers by light pollution, is breathtaking in its beauty. When primitive people gazed heavenwards, they could see at most a few thousand stars – a serene and limited universe. But now science has revealed a universe of unimaginable size, with billions of stars. The *nearest* star to the sun (Proxima Centauri) is 4.2 light years (25 million million miles) away. The sun with its planets is a tiny part of the Milky Way galaxy, a rotating group of hundreds of billions of stars. Our galaxy was once thought to be the entire universe, until discoveries in the 1920s. We now know that it is only one of a huge cluster of galaxies, which itself is part of a supercluster, which in turn is one among many. The most distant objects observed are quasars (probably the nuclei of galaxies in formation). Because their light has travelled for billions of years to reach us, to observe such phenomena is to look back in time towards the 'Big Bang' itself.

For many decades most cosmologists held firmly to the 'Steady State' view of the universe – namely that it has always 'been there', essentially unchanging. But this seemed to many at odds with biblical teaching about the creation of the world. In fact, it was only after the implications of Einstein's theory of relativity were understood that the notion of an expanding universe which had a beginning (the 'Big Bang') and may have an end (the 'Big Crunch') replaced the prevailing view. In his popular book *A Brief History Of Time* (Bantam, 1988) Professor Stephen Hawking (one of the world's leading cosmologists and widely regarded as the most brilliant theoretical physicist since Einstein) explained that after he and the mathematician and physicist Roger Penrose had written a joint paper on the subject, 'nowadays nearly everyone assumes that the universe started with a big bang singularity' (p. 50). It is fascinating to note that a scholar of the thirteenth century (Moses Nahman) observed in his 'Commentary on Genesis': 'At the briefest instant following creation all the matter of the universe was concentrated in a very small place, no larger than a grain of mustard.'

While views and information about the universe are enthralling for many people, others feel daunted and overwhelmed. Some even begin to question their faith. Perhaps they echo the words of the English poet, John Donne (1573–1631), describing his feelings about the revolutionary teachings of Copernicus, whose research proved that the sun, not the earth, was at the centre of the known 'world'. He wrote:

> The New Philosophy calls all in doubt,
> The Element of fire is quite put out;
> The Sun is lost, and th'Earth, and no man's wit

Can well direct him where to look for it . . .
'Tis all in pieces, all coherence gone;
All just supply, and all Relation.

Those who feel insecure when thinking about the big questions of the universe may prefer to consider the more immediate wonders of nature: the patterns of snowflakes; the song of birds; the colours of butterflies; the beauty of flowers and trees; the landscapes of hills and valleys; the ever-changing seas and cloud formations; the wonders of the animal kingdom; the beauty of the human body. Yet it was no more 'difficult' (to speak in human terms) for the God of the entire universe to issue the command which flung huge stars of immense energy into the vastness of space, than to create the human brain in all its unfathomable complexity. The immensity and intricacy of the universe are equally awe-inspiring. The poet Robert Fox regarded the telescope and the microscope as 'two instruments of nearly equal hope'. But, he concluded, neither has the answer:

We dance around in a ring and suppose
But the Secret sits in the middle and knows.

Back to the Bible

When looking at what the Scriptures teach about both the beginning and the end of the world, we need to bear in mind that we are not dealing with a scientific text-book. Rather, the Bible is a collection of sixty-six books of different types of literature including poetry, narrative, history, prophecy (often couched in dramatic language) and letters to young churches about doctrine and practice. It was written in three languages, over a period of some 1,400 years by over forty authors, who themselves drew upon other sources. The list, or canon, of Old Testament books was probably finally decided on by Jewish religious leaders by the end of the first century AD. Most of the New Testament, written in the first century AD, came to be accepted by the early Church by AD 130 as on a level with the Old Testament, although it was not until a Council of Rome in

AD 382 that the canon of Scripture (the Bible), as we know it today, was officially settled. God the Holy Spirit so overruled this entire process from the first book being written to the final decision about which books the Church recognised as authoritative, that it is nothing short of a major miracle that this diverse collection of books actually conveys an unfolding and unified message. The sixth Article of Faith for the Church of England describes what that is. 'Holy Scripture containeth all things necessary to salvation . . . In the name of the holy scripture we do understand those canonical Books of the Old and New Testament, of whose authority was never any doubt in the Church.'

The Bible was not inscribed supernaturally by the finger of God – that claim is only made about the ten commandments (Exod. 31:18). Rather, it is the result of dynamic interaction between God and man. That should not be too difficult to grasp, since that is what the Christian life, and to some extent the whole of life, is about. God did not obliterate human weaknesses of the writers of the Scriptures, because that is not his way. Rather, he chose to reveal his sovereignty and power through the humanity of the biblical writers. The Holy Spirit was watching over the compilation, editing, writing and choosing of these remarkable sixty-six books, with the glorious purpose in mind of conveying the word of God to humanity. These Scriptures ultimately point to *the* Word of God – Jesus.

If the Bible is not a scientific text-book, how valid is it to look for answers about how everything began and how it will all end? As we have seen, science addresses the question 'How?' (and it is important to stress that theories are often partial or provisional, and whereas some prove to be accurate, others sometimes eventually prove to be mistaken). Religion in general is more concerned with the question 'Why?' Christianity in particular is more concerned with the question 'Who?' But that does not mean that we can dismiss those aspects of Scripture which relate to history, whether recent to the writer or far back in time. After all, Jesus is the Lord of history.

Of course, it is important to assess when reading a particular book or chapter of the Bible, whether the writer is using poetic or more literal language. We need to understand also if his aim is to convey historical facts (as, for example, Luke makes clear at the beginning of his gospel), which should then be tested if possible by historians or archaeologists. It is amazing just how many aspects have proved to be accurate, from the pomegranate design on Solomon's temple to the existence of Pontius Pilate. In fact, although there are many areas of controversy, nothing in the historical accounts in the Bible has actually been disproved, which is quite remarkable for such a collection of documents. But where there is more than one eye-witness account, for instance, different (but not necessarily conflicting) details have been recalled, as one would expect. In some cases a story is told which may not be historical – it is akin to a parable, to illustrate truths about life or God, as is probably the case with the book of Job.

Truth has many aspects, whether 'spiritual' reality, or historical, or scientific, to mention but a few. Of course, long before and ever since Pontius Pilate famously asked, 'What is truth?' that same question has been posed time and again, but has probably never received an entirely satisfactory reply. Today it is fashionable, partly because of the difficulty of providing watertight proof even of scientific theories, to regard all truth as relative and subjective. As long as a belief, theory or even world-view works (even if only for a few), and doesn't harm others, then the prevailing attitude is to live and let live. By contrast, those who believe in the God who created the entire universe, who will one day speak the word which will change that universe for ever, cannot rest content with such relativism. Truth is inextricably bound up in the Godhead, and as much as we need to know for eternal life is revealed in the person of Christ, to whom the Scriptures, in the providence of God, bear witness. Where such truth is bound up in history, we should expect a reliable account; where it is to do with pre-history, we may assume supernatural revelation; where it is about the future, we may look for prophetic inspiration.

Back to the beginning

It is important to glance back at the far distant past, before looking ahead, not least because God's purposes centre on his Son, who was (and is) the agent of creation as well as the hope for the future. When describing pre-history, as in the first three chapters of the book of Genesis, the writer uses broad brush strokes in chapters 1:1–2:3 to paint an awesome picture of creation, while conveying timeless truths about God, the development of planet Earth and creation of all the major life-forms. In chapters 2:4–3:24, the highly pictorial account focuses on the first human beings; their environment; knowledge of good and evil and the devastating consequences of choosing to disobey God. The purpose of these accounts is to convey basic truths. One of the main truths we learn from the creation story in the book of Genesis is that the power of the word of God is such that he only had to say: 'Let there be . . .' and it was so.

We are told very little about any methods God may have used, though there may well be a hint in the words: 'Let the land produce vegetation . . . Let the water teem with living creatures . . . Let the land produce living creatures'(1:11, 20, 24). We are given to understand that God intervened in the on-going process of the development of life by uttering his powerful creative word on six occasions. Some think that the famous six 'days' of creation refer to divine authorisation of stages in an on-going process (without which developments would not have taken place as they did), culminating in the creation of human beings. Those who hold this view believe that the writer was using a kind of shorthand, because we now know that the first chapter at least covers a massive time-span. Many theologians are not concerned about the actual order in Genesis, preferring to concentrate on the truth of God as Creator, whatever method, time-scale and order were involved. They believe the writer of the account used a literary structure, dividing the narrative into six 'days', mainly to emphasise the orderliness of God's creation of the earth and all its life-forms.

The horror of evil

There could be no greater contrast than between the splendid beauty of creation described in the first book of the Bible (Genesis) and the ghastly horror of the end of the present order, conveyed in the last book of the Bible (Revelation). It is impossible to understand why there should be such a terrible contrast, without an awareness of the devastation brought about through human sin. The story is one of unsurpassed drama, focusing on God's plans for the earth and its inhabitants. In fact, the Genesis account concentrates almost entirely on the creation of the earth, not the whole universe. Unfortunately, it does not satisfy our keen interest to know whether or not there is life on other planets elsewhere in the universe! However, there are many fascinating references in the Bible to other types of beings of a different order to living creatures on earth. Some are called angels and archangels, others cherubim and seraphim, who worship and serve God in various ways. There are also evil beings: the devil and his minions. We know all these beings existed before human beings, because they figure in the Garden of Eden story. It is possible they were created before the earth came into existence. They are of a different order from anything in the natural world as we know it, because they do not appear to be constrained by the 'laws' of physics as we understand them.

It is significant to note that, since Satan was there in the Garden of Eden in the form of a serpent (Gen. 3:1–5; Rev. 12:9), evil was already present in the universe – it was not just introduced through the 'fall' of human beings. 'The devil has been sinning from the beginning', we read in 1 John 3:8. The Bible gives little insight into the origin of evil, except that it was connected with pride, which turned into rebellion in the mind of Satan. We can only speculate that when the devil, originally created as a true angel of light, first disobeyed God, the consequences were so disastrous that they brought disorder which may have afflicted the whole of creation, even before human beings sinned. Some scholars believe that this rebellion is referred to in Isaiah 14:12–15, even though the overt reference is to a human king. The double reference is certainly the case in Ezekiel 28:1–19.

The extent of disarray in the rest of creation, prior to the ravages resulting from human sin, should not, however, be exaggerated. Much of creation is either inanimate or incapable, it seems, of experiencing pain. Obviously, there are many animals who do suffer pain, but they probably exist from day to day, free from self-awareness, which leads to the introspective agony of thought which accounts for much human suffering, as men and women reflect on their lot in life. Even so, the savagery which can be observed in nature, which admittedly appears to be essential for the food chain, must be a long way from the perfection achieved by God, when he pronounced his creation 'very good' (Gen. 1:31). Although it is impossible for us to understand how the biological order might have been different, we do know that God has promised that perfection will be restored in the future: ' "The wolf and the lamb will feed together, and the lion will eat straw like the ox . . . They will neither harm nor destroy on all my holy mountain," says the Lord' (Isa. 65:25).

Human beings would have been protected by God from the devil and any influence of evil, if they had not fallen to temptation. The consequences were terrible, resulting in most of the misery in the world. From that point on, the backdrop to the entire Bible is of a titanic conflict being waged between spiritual forces of good and evil. Yet it is made clear throughout that God is the only Creator, the only sovereign Lord: his authority, power and victory are never in any doubt, and the only power which the devil has is whatever limited authority is permitted by God. Although in terms of the entire universe that might be miniscule, in terms of the earth it appears considerable, because 'the whole world is under the control of the evil one' (1 John 5:19).

The hope of salvation

From the point at which human beings ruined the wonderful purposes God had in store for them, the Holy Spirit inspires the biblical writers to relate the story of God the Father's extraordinary rescue plan, which encompasses human history from the very beginning to a glorious eternity. That is why the

Bible is intrinsically a prophetic book.

It is but a small thing for the Creator God, who transcends space and time, to reveal a glimpse of the future, as well as pre-history, to prophets he has gifted for this purpose. He never does this just to satisfy curiosity, but with a far greater aim in mind. The entire Bible is prophetic in the sense that as well as proclaiming God to us now, in his nature and present purposes, it also points forward to what God has in store. God had originally intended that men and women should walk and talk with him in an unbroken relationship of love. Once that was marred by sin, there was no other solution than reconciliation initiated by God. As soon as the original, tragic fall from grace had occurred, the God of revelation began to prepare the human race for his great plan of salvation: even in Genesis, there is a reference to the serpent being crushed (3:15). At the heart of the divine purpose is the Son of God, who made the greatest sacrifice of all time, to save human beings from the power of evil. This is the pivotal point of the Bible. Jesus said to his critics: 'You diligently study the Scriptures because you think that by them you possess eternal life. These are the Scriptures that testify about me, yet you refuse to come to me to have life' (John 5:39–40). So those who are dismissive of any prophetic aspect to the Scriptures have failed to grasp their purpose.

We know that the Old Testament, and the gospel narratives, point forward – to the cross. But God's purposes for future salvation did not even come to an end at the cross, resurrection and ascension, wonderful though these events were in making possible the reconciliation of God and man. Jesus accomplished all that was necessary for our salvation, bearing our sin and its penalty of separation from God the Father, rising and ascending in victory, requiring only a wholehearted response of repentance, faith and love from individuals. Yet there was, and is, more to come! There was further fulfilment of prophecy in the outpouring of the Holy Spirit on the people of God (Acts 2:1–21) so that they could continue the work of Jesus. But this was only the beginning of what is known as 'the Last Days'. If so much prophecy has already been fulfilled, we may rely on prophecies about the future.

Back to the future

Just as the Old Testament pointed forward to the coming of the Messiah (Christ), so the New Testament, having described his coming, points to the time beyond time, when God's plan of salvation will be fully realised in glory, beyond the grave – in fact, beyond the time-span for Earth as we know it. One-ninth of the New Testament refers specifically to the topics covered in this book (known as the subject of eschatology). There is also a wealth of material which is directly related. Jesus himself prophesied at length about the future, and there are prophetic passages, varying from short paragraphs to whole chapters, in all the books of the New Testament, with the exception of the short epistles of Philemon and 3 John. There is even a whole book devoted to prophecy: the book of Revelation. Some of this prophecy is couched in lurid picture language; elsewhere it is very matter-of-fact. Throughout all this teaching, it is emphasised that it is not *what* will happen that really matters, or *where*, or even *why*. The emphasis is on *who*. In other words, Jesus, the second person of the Trinity, is central – he is 'the Alpha and the Omega, the First and the Last, the Beginning and the End' (Rev. 22:13). In one sense, the entire Bible is pointing forward to the time when God will perfectly reconcile the whole world through Christ (Col. 1:15–20). He was not only the agent of creation, but the promise of God for the future. That is why so much of the Bible is about the end, as well as about the beginning and the present.

The future of planet Earth

First the bad news: in considering the prophetic teaching in the Bible about events still in the future, we shall first look ahead to the end of the age: the end of time itself, as we know it. The events now to be described occur *after* the Second Coming of Christ. Although other very disturbing events affecting the earth are outlined in a number of passages of Scripture, they are concerned with the time between the two comings of Jesus. We shall consider those later. There are only a few references to the final scenario, but it becomes painfully clear that, although ultimately there is good news for the earth, that will only be fulfilled after terrible destruction.

One of the most striking verses is 2 Peter 3:10: 'But the day of the Lord will come like a thief. The heavens will disappear with a roar; the elements will be destroyed by fire, and the earth and everything in it will be laid bare.' Another such description is to be found in the book of Revelation. Having described all kinds of trials, including persecution, which the people of God would be called upon to endure down through the centuries, the writer moves on to deal with final end-time events, including the destruction of the devil himself. After that he 'saw a great white throne and him who was seated on it. Earth and sky fled from his presence, and there was no place for them' (20:11). 'Then I saw a new heaven and a new earth, for the first earth had passed away, and there was no longer any sea' (21:1).

Although there can be no doubt that some prophetic passages of Scripture use extreme language to convey God's judgments, it is difficult from the context of these two references to draw any other conclusion than that St Peter and St John, inspired by the Holy Spirit, were foretelling a cataclysmic event which, in the sovereign timing of God, is going to overwhelm planet Earth. The almighty God only has to speak the word to create or destroy. But we have amply demonstrated that, whereas previous generations of Christians might have thought of this as occurring in a completely 'supernatural' way, there is abundant scientific research today to show that such destruction could take place as a result, for example, of an asteroid collision. The supernatural element would then be in the timing (although, since God is the Creator, it is a false distinction, in many ways, to contrast 'natural' and 'supernatural'). An article in *New Scientist* (New Science Publications, 27 June 1998) began with these words:

ARMAGEDDON STRIKES. Perhaps it comes in the shape of a nuclear war, or a new virus – deadlier than AIDS and more infectious than the common cold – or a collision with a huge meteorite. Whatever the cause, imagine that *Homo Sapiens* suddenly passes into history. It's a shocking scenario, but perfectly plausible – witness the demise of the dinosaurs 65 million years ago . . . Today, we are rulers of the planet. A hundred million years from now, will we just be history?

We may at least draw comfort from the belief that the destruction of humanity, or the earth, or both, will not take place *before* God speaks the word.

Why would the God who lovingly created the earth allow such a final catastrophe to destroy it? If *we* love this planet in all its beauty, with its fascinating variety of life, its stunning landscapes, its vast oceans and splendid resources, how much more does God? How it will grieve him when the time comes to speak, not a life-giving word, nor even a redemptive word of warning, but the final word of judgment. Why would he do that? It could only be that the accumulation of man's inhumanity to man will have reached saturation point, such that the suffering of the majority means that life for them is no longer endurable, let alone enjoyable. Not only that, but the earth may well have been so ravaged and laid waste by those who were meant to nurture it and use its resources wisely and fairly, that it has become a scene of plunder rather than plenty.

The thought of destruction on such a massive scale is so horrendous that we need to know: will there be any human beings living on the earth at that stage to witness and be a part of its demise? That is an issue which will be explored later. We are given few clues as to when this terrible disaster will overwhelm the earth, except that it will be after the return of Christ. But we do know that it will mean not only the end of one era, but the beginning of the next: God has prepared a glorious future beyond this catastrophe.

Chapter 2

Is there life after life?

'Then I saw a new heaven and a new earth.'

(Rev. 21:1)

The good news

God has in store a New World Order which far surpasses any utopia planned by men and women. The Creator God, who planned the first earth, will speak into being a new earth, complete with new life-forms: there will be a link with previous existence, but only comparable to the relationship of plants to seeds. Here is one description:

Then I saw a new heaven and a new earth . . . And I heard a loud voice from the throne saying, 'Now the dwelling of God is with men, and he will live with them. They will be his people, and God himself will be with them and be their God. He will wipe every tear from their eyes. There will be no more death or mourning or crying or pain, for the old order of things has passed away.' (Rev. 21:1, 3–4).

These verses turn upside down the idea which most people have of heaven. Instead of whisking people away to some ethereal place, God actually creates a new earth, where he will dwell with his people. He will not, of course, be confined to the new earth, because he is not limited even to the vastness of the whole universe, but his presence on earth will be tangible. 'Heaven' will be on earth!

But does God 'resurrect' the old earth, which will have suffered massive destruction, re-creating it so that it is fit for him to dwell with those he has redeemed, and if so, how extensive is the restoration? That all depends, of course, on the extent of the destruction, which marks the end of this age. Some think the earth will only require renewal. Others take the references quoted at the end of the last chapter as meaning literal, total devastation, so that the earth is unrecognisable – even becoming a fireball, or blown apart into fragments of matter. Either way, most scholars believe God takes what is left, lovingly making it new, because he is in the restoration business! However, a different scenario is possible. There is an interesting verse in 2 Peter 3:7: 'the present heavens and earth are reserved for fire, being kept for the day of judgment and destruction of ungodly men.' It could be that the future of the present earth is tied up with the destiny of the ungodly, whereas God creates an entirely new 'earth' for the habitation of those who have trusted him in this life.

Some may be wondering why St John in his vision saw a new heaven as well as a new earth, if heaven will in fact be 'on' the new earth. In the Hebrew language, the same plural word is used for what we would call 'the heavens', meaning 'the skies', and 'heaven', meaning the abode of God. That is probably because the Jewish people thought of God as living above the observable sky. So here, it may refer to God creating new skies – in other words, God might transform the whole universe – *or* it may mean the new earth will be in a different position in the universe (therefore the observable skies are 'new' to the earth). Another possibility is that it could mean some renewal of the solar system, so that there are no dangers from asteroids, for instance, for the renewed earth. *Or* it could mean some transformation in the abode of God, such that there would be no possibility of the rebellion which brought about the fall of the mighty angel who became the devil.

More about the new earth

Its central characteristic is the closeness of the presence of God. Picture language is used in the book of Revelation, of a beautiful city shining with the presence of God. It does not need the light of the sun or moon, 'for the glory of God gives it light, and the Lamb is its lamp' (Rev. 21:23). Here we live by faith; there we shall be able to see God 'face to face' (1 Cor. 13:12). Certainly we shall be able to walk and talk with the risen Jesus, who has gone on ahead to prepare a place for believers. In John 14:3 we read that he promised: 'I will come back and take you to be with me that you also may be where I am.' It is difficult to envisage what it will be like vividly to *experience* the presence of God all the time. In this life, emotions are fickle, affected so often by circumstances or physical state. For most people an experience of God is rare, or, when it does occur, it can be rather like looking through frosted glass. However, on occasions an intense awareness of the presence of God can be exquisite, surpassing even the most special moments of human love, or the depth of feeling which some sense when losing themselves in the wonders of nature. It should not require too much imagination to begin to appreciate just how indescribably wonderful heaven will be.

There is so much emphasis in modern life on the 'feel-good factor' that for many the search for it dominates their lives. For some it is so elusive that they resort to drugs, even in the knowledge that elation will invariably be followed by depression, nightmares and, ultimately, physical and mental damage. There has been greater emphasis more recently on the 'highs' of spiritual experiences, achieved through meditation, for example, as people search for meaning and fulfilment. But it is only in heaven that the true secret of a fulfilled life will be completely understood. Jesus spelt it out two thousand years ago: 'Whoever finds his life will lose it, and whoever loses his life for my sake will find it' (Matt. 10:39). In heaven we shall totally lose ourselves in love, worship and service to God, which will result in discovering the true meaning of life, the by-product of which happens to be fulfilment.

There is a problem. It is clear in the Scriptures that we cannot love God without loving others, and to love people with God's love is to serve them sacrificially. Those who do that, albeit imperfectly in this life, may experience all kinds of trials, but they are more fulfilled than all those who chase after happiness for selfish reasons. But, although we have no problem imagining that we shall feel love towards others in the next life, how will it be possible to serve them, if they have no needs? It is probable that God has planned ways of serving him which are to do with the ordering of life on the new earth (and some would like to think that if there is life elsewhere in the universe, there will be responsibilities in that connection. But that is only supposition.). There are likely to be opportunities to show our God-given love for others, as each person fulfils a role for the good of the whole.

Feelings, of course, are not everything. Knowledge is very important to being human. How amazing it will be to find that we 'just know' the answers to all the questions ever asked. Perhaps this knowledge will be revealed progressively, throughout eternity. 'Now I know in part; then I shall know fully, even as I am fully known' (1 Cor. 13:12). That verse refers primarily to 'the light of the knowledge of the glory of God in the face of Christ' (2 Cor. 4:6), but we may speculate that God would want to give his children knowledge of the universe too.

Heaven on earth will be far removed from the spooky state which so many people imagine. Since there will be no suffering, the sense of reality is likely to be more intense than in our present existence. In the absence of any pain or weakness, we shall be more truly alive than is possible in this life. Here, physical or mental ailments can dull our senses, or our body chemistry may not function on full power, or our circumstances may be difficult, or relationships problematic, or we feel frustrated because we lack the time or ability to learn all that we would love to know about life, the universe and everything. In heaven there will be no such disadvantages.

A suitable environment

The new earth will be created by God in such a way as to be suitable for people with bodies which have been resurrected and re-created. We shall consider the resurrection in more detail later. We know from the gospels that Jesus could appear and disappear at will, but it is difficult to imagine how this could be, with our present knowledge of physics. Yet it is not only the human body which will be radically different. It soon becomes obvious from further study that the new earth cannot just be a restoration of the old to its former state (except that it will be untarnished by human sin). After all, the passage in Revelation chapter 21 reveals that there will be no more suffering, weeping or death, 'for the old order of things has passed away'. Yet, as touched on in the first chapter, the more we get to know about the present eco-system, the more we realise that every form of insect, reptile, bird, fish and mammal life lives by feeding off either vegetation or micro-organisms or other species. If *all* suffering (not just that of human beings) comes to an end, it is impossible to underestimate the massive changes which would be involved in the old order making way for the new.

Perhaps some of the possibilities are hinted at in the book of Isaiah, in the writer's vision of new heavens and a new earth: 'The former things will not be remembered, nor will they come to mind ... They will neither harm nor destroy on all my holy mountain, says the Lord' (Isa. 65:17, 25). In the New Testament, St Paul writes that 'the creation itself will be liberated from its bondage to decay and brought into the glorious freedom of the children of God' (Rom. 8:21). When all the implications are thought through, it no longer seems credible to think of a superficial renewal of the earth – 'just' deleting the consequences of human sin and all trace of the final judgment which God visited on the planet, wonderful though the absence of those factors would be. After all, by this time the presence of evil will have been totally eradicated: not just human sin, terrible though that is, but the devil himself (Rev. 20:10) and death (1 Cor. 15:26). If this means there will be no death at all in the whole of the new created order, a more radical transformation is called for, with possibly new laws of physics, chemistry and biology. Such concepts may even be irrelevant when considering life in a new dimension. At the very least, there will be a restoration to the perfect state of creation before it was affected by the intrusion of evil into the universe.

In the book of Revelation, the apostle John records that he not only saw the new heaven and earth, but that the first heaven and earth had passed away. Some think that God will radically redesign, at the same time as restoring, the present earth. Others think that a new 'earth' will be established somewhere else in the universe as we know it, in the belief that totally different conditions of life might be able to operate in a vastly different environment. Or what God has in store might be another 'world' which either interacts with or totally supersedes the present order. In any event, it is likely that God will use something of the old matter, just as he will do when raising human bodies, to demonstrate his re-affirmation of his original perfect creation and his redemptive power. But the weight of the following words should not be underestimated: 'He who was seated on the throne said, "I am making everything new! . . . these words are trustworthy and true" ' (Rev. 21:5).

Heaven, before the destruction of earth

If, after the Last Judgment, heaven will be on the new earth, where is it *now*? The average person thinks of it in some mysterious location 'above the bright blue sky', where they imagine God to be. But since God is Spirit (John 4:24), it is unlikely that he requires 'place' as we understand it. The thousands of angels who encircle the 'throne', worshipping God (Rev. 5:11), are also spirits, but of a lesser order (Heb. 1:14). They are not divine, but were created to minister to God, and eventually to human beings. It is reasonable to suppose that the angels of God inhabit a universe of a different order from the one we know, which interacts with the space–time universe, in ways which are largely hidden from our knowledge. At the same time God pervades the created world. We learn that no one can escape the presence of God (Ps. 139:5–12). God shows his sovereignty over and within the created order; he guides all those he has created, seeking to bless them, to draw out sacrificial love, good deeds and creativity which is honouring to him; he judges evil, sometimes in this life; he draws people to himself in faith, love and worship; he answers prayer; he heals; he guides – to name but a few of the ways in which many experience God in this life. He sometimes even permits a manifestation of himself, apparent to the sense of sight or hearing. For example, Jacob wrestled with a 'man' whom he later recognised to be God (Gen. 32:22–32). Moses was permitted to see God, but not his face (Exod. 33:21–3). There are other examples in Scripture, which are more than visions (normally it is made clear in Scripture as to whether someone is having a dream, or experiencing a vision or a real event). One of the most dramatic examples is described in the book of Daniel, when the three men who were thrown into the furnace were not only supernaturally protected, but joined by one who looked like 'a son of the gods' (Dan. 3:19–30). It is possible that these encounters were with a manifestation of God the Son, before the incarnation, because in several places in the Bible we learn that no one has seen God the Father. For example, in St John's gospel we read: 'No-one has ever seen God, but God the One and Only, who is at the Father's side, has made him known' (John 1:18). There are also numerous examples of angels appearing to human beings. One incident seems to indicate they are all around us, if only we have eyes to see (2 Kgs. 6:15–17).

When it comes to the interaction of God with men the supreme example is that of the incarnate Son of God, who lived on this earth for over thirty years. The second person of the Trinity took human form, humbling himself, even to death on a cross (Phil. 2:6–13). St John said of his Lord: 'That which was from the beginning, which we have heard, which we have seen with our eyes, which we have looked at and our hands have touched – this we proclaim concerning the Word of life' (1 John 1:1). As for the third person of the Trinity, until the time of the ascension of Christ only a chosen few had been filled by the power of the Holy Spirit. After that, from the Day of Pentecost, God chose to interact so closely with every believer that it is possible for all those who trust in Christ, without exception, to be filled with the power of the Holy Spirit.

In these ways, and many more, heaven and the angels are seen to be all around us and God even indwells his children. Although words like '*up*' are often used in Scripture in connection with heaven, that is because the Holy Spirit did not override the world view of biblical authors, who thought of the abode of God as above the earth, and the abode of the dead below. It was not relevant to God's main purpose at the time the New Testament was written to change this view, which tied in with the knowledge available at that time. It is true that, at the ascension, Jesus 'was taken *up* . . . and a cloud hid him' (Acts 1:9), but only such a dramatic finale would have convinced the disciples that the earthly ministry of Jesus had come to a close. It is more likely he passed into another dimension.

The in-between state

If heaven in the future will be on the new earth, but in the present is in another dimension all around us, one of the main questions which people are bound to ask is: does that mean that those who have died are all around us as well? Some would want to answer 'Yes'. Others would want to add that while their spirits inhabit the unseen universe, they are not aware of what is happening on earth. (We can only speculate that if ghosts are anything more than a figment of the imagination, they are either troubled human spirits, which have not made the full transition, or demonic counterfeits.) A different answer as to where human spirits go after this life is that death ushers them into a new dimension, where not only is space irrelevant, but also time (both being inextricably linked, as modern physics has demonstrated). From the point of view of those who have died, there may well be no time-lapse between the experience of death and being raised at the Second Coming. However, physicists and some modern philosophers would regard it as impossible to exist outside of time. It might be more a matter that awareness of passage of time is relative, and could become meaningless. Everyone knows that to watch the clock impatiently for time to move quickly seems to make it slow down, and the reverse is also true. If there is no end to a state of being, but rather a perpetual 'now', that is virtually the same as to escape time altogether.

No believer need fear the 'in-between' existence. It was a major concern of many Old Testament writers, who dreaded 'Sheol', the abode of the dead, but that was because none except the later writers had any understanding of resurrection (with the possible exception of the writer of the book of Job). There are hints in the New Testament that existence prior to the Last Judgment will not be comfortable for unbelievers. Jesus told a vivid parable of the anguish experienced by an uncaring rich man after his death (Luke 16:19–31), and St Peter refers to 'continuing their punishment' before Judgment Day (2 Pet. 2:9). But in the New Testament it becomes clear that, prior to the resurrection, those who have believed in God's revelation in this life are secure 'in Christ'. It may well be that the next event of which they become aware will be the return of Christ. Then God will create heaven on earth for his children, after the Last Judgment. As our loving heavenly Father, he wants us to be excited and thrilled by such a prospect, even if over-awed and naturally apprehensive. He intended that we should live in the light of all that is in store for us. 'No eye has seen, no ear has heard, no mind has conceived what God has prepared for those who love him' (1 Cor. 2:9).

Heaven here and now

We have considered where heaven is after the Last Judgment, where heaven (the abode of the angels) is now, and the whereabouts of those 'in Christ' before the Second Coming. But there is a sense in which heaven can be experienced *in the present*. God intended originally that we should experience his close presence on earth, as pictured in the Garden of Eden. When that plan was marred by sin, he began lovingly to reveal his plan of salvation (which, paradoxically, he had planned from before the foundation of the world), so that his purpose of dwelling with human beings could be fulfilled even more gloriously in the future. Although no one will experience the perfection of

God's plan until the new heaven and new earth are created, he intends that his children should begin to experience it here and now. That is why Jesus said 'You must be born again' (John 3:7). God's plan was that 'whoever believes in [Jesus] shall not perish but *have* eternal life' (John 3:16). Very often when people put their trust in Jesus for the first time, they experience a glimpse of heaven. They feel more alive; they view creation with new eyes; there is an awareness of the presence of God; his word in the Bible seems to be written just for them; there is a new understanding of God's ways; life takes on a sense of purpose. After a while the acuteness of the sense of newness begins to dim, as God intended that we should live by faith, not feelings. But every now and then, similar experiences recur. In particular, it is possible to experience the presence of God fairly often, when involved regularly in corporate worship. Meanwhile, an on-going process of becoming more like Jesus should be taking place, such that we become less self-centred, increasingly filled with love for God and able to serve others with sacrificial love. Issues of justice, human rights and ways of meeting the needs of those less fortunate than ourselves begin to assume greater importance. It is also the responsibility of human beings to care for this planet, which, despite damage already inflicted, is such a special place. Above all, those transformed by Christ will want to encourage that transformation in others. In these ways, something of God's will is done on earth as in heaven – in fact, heaven may be glimpsed on earth here and now, even where light and darkness co-exist. It is possible to experience wonderful joy in this life, but, sadly, death casts a long shadow over its pleasures.

The shadow of death

It is an inescapable fact that death is the only certain event in life. But even though we live in an age when, through television and films, more people are exposed to images of death than ever before, there is greater reluctance to discuss the subject. Yet its lurking presence dominates life, whether there is conscious awareness of that or not. Many people suppress any thought of death, because they are so terrified by it. Their feelings on the subject have been superbly described by Shakespeare in *Measure for Measure*:

> Death is a fearful thing . . .
> Ay, but to die, and go we know not where;
> To lie in cold obstruction, and to rot;
> This sensible warm motion to become
> A kneaded clod; and the delighted spirit
> To bathe in fiery floods . . . 'tis too horrible!
> The weariest and most loathed worldly life
> That age, ache, penury, and imprisonment
> Can lay on nature, is a paradise
> To what we fear of death.

Even those who firmly believe they are destined for heaven entertain understandable fears of embarking on this ultimate journey, with its one-way ticket. Most fear the process of dying, lest it be drawn-out and painful. There is concern for family members; dread at the prospect of leaving loved ones behind, together with all that is familiar and appreciated in this life. But, in addition, we have been furnished with so few details of what to expect, either as we travel or about our destination. Even though we may look forward to the wonderful life which God has prepared for us after the close of this age, the dark tunnel of death itself still has to be negotiated. Surely only those whose life is intolerable actually welcome death, unless a person has lived a long life, become frail, and is able to regard death as a release.

Paradoxically, the knowledge that life on this earth is limited may have advantages. For those who are willing to face reality, this knowledge concentrates the mind, bringing about a determination to make the most of the time available. It inspires some to make a positive contribution to the value of this life, and, coupled with an unselfish attitude, may lead to a more urgent desire to further the well-being of others. Fear of death, or its sudden closeness, may cause some to choose eternal life in Christ.

God is able to use to good purpose the reality that all face death, just as he enables those with a right heart-attitude to triumph in suffering. Even so, death itself is regarded in the Scriptures as an enemy. In fact it is the judgment of God on sin. Adam was warned: 'You must not eat from the tree of the knowledge of good and evil, for when you eat of it you will surely die' (Gen. 2:17). Tragically, both Adam and Eve rebelled against their Creator. The consequences for the human race are spelt out in Romans 5:12: 'sin entered the world through one man, and death through sin, and in this way death came to all men, because all sinned.'

This poses several problems. If there had been no sin, would human beings not have died, but remained on the earth? If so, surely it would have become rather crowded! In any case, it seems that all other living creatures experience death as part of the natural cycle, following birth and reproduction. If human beings were born to die after all, some scholars think what is meant in Romans 5:12, and elsewhere, is spiritual death, i.e. separation from God. In our view it is more likely that God originally intended men and women to live in a beautiful world, enjoying his creation and his presence (perhaps for much longer than 'three score years and ten'), but then he planned simply to take them into his nearer presence, without experiencing a death process. In fact, this seems to have happened to two people mentioned in the Bible. One was Enoch, who 'walked with God; then he was no more, because God took him away' (Gen. 5:24). A more dramatic whisking away happened to Elijah (2 Kgs. 2:11). Apart from that, all face death. That is why the resurrection of Christ is so important.

Resurrection: God's solution to death

God chose the death and resurrection of his Son to defeat death. Who but God could have planned such a solution? There could be no better example of the truth that his ways are not our ways, for his thoughts are higher than our thoughts (Isa. 55:8–9). God himself cannot die, but when his Son came into the world, as a result of the union of divine and human nature, a unique sin-bearing death was possible. The ultimate judgment upon sin – separation between God and a human being – was borne, when

God the Son cried out just before he died to God the Father: 'My God, my God, why have you forsaken me?' (Matt. 27:46). But God had planned by his mighty power to raise him on the third day, dealing a death-blow to death itself. 'Christ Jesus . . . has destroyed death and has brought life and immortality to light through the gospel' (2 Tim. 1:10).

Why then do believers still experience death? It is made clear in Hebrews 2:14–15 that the *power* and *fear* of death have been destroyed by Jesus: 'he too shared in their humanity so that by his death he might destroy him who holds the power of death – that is, the devil – and free those who all their lives were held in slavery by their fear of death.' But it is only after death that believers experience freedom from death, and only at the Second Coming of Christ that the results of the victory won two thousand years ago will be fully realised. 'Christ, the firstfruits; then, when he comes, those who belong to him. Then the end will come . . . The last enemy to be destroyed is death' (1 Cor. 15:23–6). But meanwhile, even though most believers would not say they look forward to dying, they can echo the words of St Paul in 1 Corinthians 15:55:

> Where, O death, is your victory?
> Where, O death, is your sting?

With the glorious hope of everlasting life before us (the biblical meaning of the word for 'hope' is not weak wishful thinking, but an assured confidence in God), surely Christians ought to be less hesitant about preparing people for death and the after-life? We may not know the answers to every question, but there is enough teaching in Scripture to inform our faith. Furthermore, the testimony of some believers actually facing death should inspire us. We know of a clergyman who had a near-death experience after he was thought to be terminally ill. He lived to tell of what it had been like to pass through the valley of the shadow of death. He spoke of a sense of nearing home, and a strong awareness of a warm welcome to the life beyond awaiting him. We remember a woman in her early seventies, dying of cancer, who was a joy to visit, because her radiant faith shone through her suffering. Both these Christians based their hope for the future on the promises of God in Scripture.

Firm belief in what is to come should also transform life here and now. It should motivate believers to share their faith with others; encourage a sense of purpose; and bring comfort in difficult circumstances. Above all, belief in the resurrection of Jesus should prove a constant inspiration, to live life filled with his power.

Resurrection: God's guarantee of the next life

The importance of the resurrection of Christ is usually underestimated, even by Christians who celebrate it every year. It was not only God's 'Amen' to the sin-bearing death of his Son on the cross, vital though that was. It was, as we have seen, a powerful victory, providing the final solution to the dark triumvirate of sin, death and hell. But it was more. *Jesus, clothed in his risen body, was, and is, the foretaste of God's new creation, which will be revealed in all its glory when God raises human beings from the dead, and creates a new heaven and earth*. Although there are a handful of examples recorded in the Bible of amazing miracles when people were brought back to life, the resurrection of Jesus is in a different category altogether. People such as Jairus' daughter, or Lazarus, were restored to normal existence in this life, whether a short time after death or after four days in the tomb. In due course these people died again. But God clothed Jesus in a risen body, which is indestructible. It is clear that, for the New Testament writers, this glorious truth totally transformed their view of the after-life, filling them with anticipation as to what God had in store for them.

The gospels provide us with considerable information about Jesus after he rose from the dead. We discover that he could appear or disappear; that sometimes he was clearly recognisable, while at other times it was not immediately obvious that it was Jesus; he could behave with apparent normality, such as eating a meal; he showed concern for his disciples; he taught them further truths about God's purposes. He made it clear he was not a ghost, and showed his disciples the marks of his wounds. (That does not necessarily mean that wounds, scars or other defacing marks will remain on the bodies of people when resurrected – in the case of Jesus they serve as an important visual reminder throughout eternity of his death on the cross for the sins of the world.)

As for the new bodies of believers, there is extensive teaching on the subject in the Bible. It is clear that the resurrection of Jesus was a 'first' in God's purposes, to be followed by the resurrection of all human beings, after which God creates the new heavens and earth. The wonderful truth is that we shall be 'clothed' with imperishable bodies! This is glorious news! For centuries, even millennia, men and women have been searching for the secret of immortality, including how to live for ever in this life, or, if that fails, how to preserve their bodies so that they do not decay. Some go to enormous expense to have the bodies of relatives frozen, or otherwise preserved. Apparently there is a flourishing business in the USA in mummifying bodies, developing techniques gleaned from discoveries made in Egyptian pyramids, in the hope that new medical advances will enable resuscitation and prolonged life. Vast amounts of money are also spent on research into how to add a few years to the average life-span. Indeed, in the Western world, the average has increased considerably, as health-care has improved and standards of living risen. If someone dies in their sixties or seventies (let alone even younger) it is thought that they have been cheated of a decade or two. But even to live for nearly a century is a relatively short time in the grand scheme of things. Aware of that, folk dream about life after death, concocting all manner of weird and wonderful views on the subject, from reincarnation to being snatched away by UFOs, reappearing on another planet as little green creatures. Even Christians seem ill-informed on the subject, tending to think of the next world as one where spirits float around, playing mystical music on heavenly harps.

By contrast, the biblical teaching is loud and clear: *the body is vital in God's loving purposes*. Although body, mind and spirit, or spirit, soul and body, are differentiated in Scripture, they are mentioned as aspects of the whole person. Hebrew thought is very down-to-earth and holistic. After all, God lovingly invented and created our bodies – they are important to him! Their complexity is such that medical science is still only swimming in the shallows, remarkable though advances have been, in the last hundred years in particular. It was only in the sixteenth century that the view that feelings were based in the heart was discredited (although we still speak as if that were the case). In 1543 the anatomist Andreas Vesalius showed that the mind and the seat of our feelings are in the brain, but it was not until the eighteenth and nineteenth centuries that the nature of the nervous system, and its link with the brain, began to be understood. We now know there are as many as a hundred billion individual neurons, each one connected to thousands of others, in the human brain. They constantly communicate with each other, sending up to 300 signals a second, which undergo transformations from electrical to chemical and back again. The body itself is made up of more than 50,000 billion cells, of at least 200 main kinds. Here is a universe in miniature, much of it still awaiting discovery. The Psalmist only knew a fraction when he exclaimed: 'I am fearfully and wonderfully made' (Ps. 139:14).

New bodies

Since the human body was the pinnacle of God's original creation, we shouldn't be surprised that he has decided to use it as a starting point for even more amazing developments in his new creation. As we have seen, the new body will be imperishable – no more built-in obsolescence! More details emerge in St Paul's fascinating teaching in 1 Corinthians chapter 15. Jesus was seen after his resurrection on several occasions, including by five hundred people at once. His resurrection is the guarantee of ours, and also provides us with clues about our new bodies, some of which we have noted already. Just as a seed dies before a plant can grow, so the body dies to make way for the risen body. This is as different as the plant is to the seed, yet (to use modern terminology) was contained in its code: the one dependent for its characteristics on the other. It is no longer subject to weakness, but rather 'is raised in power' (1 Cor. 15:43). Although Paul describes it as a 'spiritual' as compared with a 'natural' body, it is still a body, not 'just' a spirit! The human spirit survives the death of the body, but is clothed with the new body after the Second Coming of Christ. We shall 'bear the likeness of the man from heaven' (1 Cor. 15:49). Although the new body is not composed of flesh and blood, we know from Jesus' risen body that it can resemble the earthly body.

Some questions are probably irrelevant, such as: 'Will people look the age at which they died, and if not, how will they be recognised?' The answer is probably quite simple: we shall 'just know' who is who, and age will be irrelevant (delighting both those who worry about their age, and those who can never remember names!). We are also informed quite clearly that there is no marriage, so presumably no sexual relationships or reproduction, in heaven. Since most people think that life would in consequence be rather lacking, perhaps it would help if they ponder that the God who invented the joy of a loving, sexual union is well able to provide delights beyond our imagination. More puzzling is the matter as to what is raised of the original. The actual body of Jesus was raised from the tomb, which was found to be empty shortly afterwards. But what of those who died long ago, or whose ashes have been scattered to the winds? It would seem that God takes what is left, to honour his original creation, to defeat death, and to use as the 'genetic code' or heavenly blueprint for the resurrected person. But where there is 'nothing' left, that blueprint presumably is in the mind of God, making it irrelevant as to how much or how little of the original body remained, prior to the resurrection.

It is important to note that, just because God has planned transformation, that is not an adverse comment on his original creation. 'Matter' in itself is neither good nor evil *morally* speaking, although God regarded what he had originally created as 'good' in the sense of very special in its basic essence, wonderfully constructed and designed to bring glory to him, if his guiding principles were followed. In fact, since they have been widely flouted, one day (as we have seen) God may choose to destroy the earth utterly. At that point, God will not just refashion the old – he will translate, transmute and transform it into a new creation. This is true also of the bodies of those 'in Christ', as the following verses make clear (1 Cor. 15:42–4):

> The body that is sown is perishable,
>   it is raised imperishable;
> it is sown in dishonour,
>   it is raised in glory;
> it is sown in weakness,
>   it is raised in power;
> it is sown a natural body,
>   it is raised a spiritual body.

We learn from elsewhere in Scripture that after the resurrection, God's children will be purified of sin, all evil will be banished and everything in heaven and earth will be reconciled to God through Christ. What a glorious future God has prepared for those who love and trust him! But what does the future hold for those who have neither loved nor trusted him in this life?

Chapter 3

Is hell out of date?

'Will not the Judge of all the earth do right?'

(Gen. 18:25)

Is hell anything more than a four-letter word, or a figment of the vindictive imagination of biblical writers, perpetuated by mediaeval imagery or Victorian indoctrination? Even if one regards the lurid language of the Bible about ghastly torment, searing flames and devouring worms as pictorial, the thought of millions of people enduring everlasting punishment is revolting. It seems totally at odds with the central message of Scripture, of the God who so loved the world that he sent his Son to save it. Surely he will forgive everybody, just as he expects people to forgive each other?

That would seem the perfect solution, until we consider more carefully the crimes against humanity which have never been judged in this life – whether committed by one individual against another, or perpetrated on a vast scale. Where there is no repentance in this life, should such men as Hitler, Stalin, Pol Pot and other ruthless dictators, who exterminated or ruined the lives of millions, be allowed to go scot-free, or the abusers of defenceless children, or those who exploit the poor, the elderly, the weak? Should the person who lives an utterly self-centred life be treated by God in the same way as one who has spent a lifetime ministering to the needs of others? Should those who ignore or scoff at the God of the universe be seen in the same light as those who love, worship and serve him?

Justice and judgment

The Church in the West is, on the whole, uncomfortable with the concept of the judgment of God, preferring instead to emphasise justice. Yet it is impossible to have the one without the other! Many people have a strong, even overpowering, sense of justice about individual cases. In addition, a corporate social conscience increasingly characterises Western society in some respects, at least by comparison with bygone eras. (Unfortunately there are still some huge blind spots, including over dealing with the gap between rich and poor, within and between nations.) Many of the leading social reformers of the nineteenth and twentieth centuries were devout Christians – Wilberforce, Shaftesbury, Fry, Tutu, to name but a few – who reminded their contemporaries of the appeals of the Old Testament prophets for a just and caring society. Yet campaigning for greater justice requires not only making positive reforms, but dealing (severely if necessary) with negative elements: whether unhelpful laws, corrupt officialdom, criminals, oppressors – whatever or whoever might be hindering those developments. If this means that individuals have to be brought to book, then that nettle has to be grasped.

God is the Judge of the whole earth. We derive any sense of true justice from him. He would be failing the human race abysmally if he did not judge individuals, governments and nations – declaring innocent, vindicating and restoring where appropriate; declaring guilty and sentencing where necessary. Unlike human justice, with all its imperfections or miscarriages of justice, God's judgments will be perfect, dealing even with motives, wrong thoughts and failure to do good, as well as unhelpful or downright evil words and deeds. At all times, we need to remember that God's essential nature is love (1 John 4:16); therefore, his justice and his judgments are an aspect of that love. 'It is high time to discover the gospel of God's judgment and to awaken joy in God's coming righteousness and justice,' commented Jurgen Moltmann in his book *The Coming of God* (SCM, 1996, p. 235).

The sentences God metes out will be seen and acknowledged

to be *totally* appropriate. Something of that may be seen in this life. It is no great surprise that those who abuse their own bodies sometimes reap appalling physical consequences. People who are choked up with resentment or even hatred usually become bitter and twisted in their personalities. Yet, more often than not, life seems very unfair. The Psalmist, in his anguish, expressed it like this:

Surely God is good . . . to those who are pure in heart.
But as for me, my feet had almost slipped; I had nearly lost
  my foothold.
For I envied the arrogant when I saw the prosperity of the wicked.
They have no struggles; their bodies are healthy and strong.
They are free from the burdens common to man; they are not
  plagued by human ills.
Therefore pride is their necklace; they clothe themselves with
  violence.
From their callous hearts comes iniquity; the evil . . . of their
  minds know[s] no limits.
They scoff, and speak with malice; in their arrogance they
  threaten oppression.
Their mouths lay claim to heaven, and their tongues take
  possession of the earth.
Therefore their people turn to them and drink up waters in
  abundance.
They say, 'How can God know? Does the Most High have
  knowledge?'
This is what the wicked are like – always carefree, they increase
  in wealth.
Surely in vain have I kept my heart pure; in vain have I washed
  my hands in innocence.
All day long I have been plagued; I have been punished every
  morning.
If I had said, 'I will speak thus,' I would have betrayed your
  children.
When I tried to understand all this, it was oppressive to me
till I entered the sanctuary of God; then I understood their
  final destiny.

> Surely you place them on slippery ground; you cast them down
> to ruin.
> How suddenly are they destroyed, completely swept away by
> terrors! . . .
> When my heart was grieved and my spirit embittered,
> I was senseless and ignorant; I was a brute beast before you.
> Yet I am always with you; you hold me by my right hand.
> You guide me with your counsel, and afterwards you will take
> me into glory.
> Whom have I in heaven but you? And earth has nothing I
> desire besides you.
> My flesh and my heart may fail, but God is the strength of
> my heart . . . for ever.
> Those who are far from you will perish; you destroy all who
> are unfaithful to you.
> But as for me . . . I have made the Sovereign LORD my refuge.
> (Ps. 73)

Promises are to be found throughout Scripture that God will
one day, whether in this life or the next, vindicate the poor, the
oppressed, those treated unjustly, those with no human advocate.
He will surely come to their rescue, but he will oppose their
oppressors. Such promises are worthless if there is no Day of
Judgment: no vindication of innocent victims; no sentencing of
those who have deliberately or even thoughtlessly contributed
to the suffering of other human beings.

Salvation and judgment

Before looking at judgment in more detail, it is vital to stress
that God longs to save, rather than to pass a final verdict of
'Guilty'. *That is why God's plan of salvation through Jesus is
intended for anyone and everyone who responds in faith, trusting
him for their eternal destiny.* One of the most well-known verses
in the Bible makes this clear: 'For God so loved the world that
he gave his one and only Son, that whoever believes in him shall
not perish but have eternal life' (John 3:16). God sent his Son to
save, not to condemn. Divine love for every single person who

has ever lived is so powerful that the Holy Spirit strives with each human spirit, to bring conviction of sin, repentance and revelation of the one true God. Tragically, many ignore that voice of the Holy Spirit, whether it is spoken through conscience, whispered Spirit to spirit, or shouted through dramatic circumstances in the life of an individual.

Yet no one escapes the Day of Judgment – neither those who ignore or quench the Spirit nor even those who respond positively to God's hidden work in their lives. Everyone – believer and unbeliever alike – will have to stand before Christ on the final Judgment Day. That will take place after the Second Coming and the resurrection of the dead. Those who have believed in this life will be granted eternal life in 'heaven on earth'. That verdict will be the confirmation of a transaction between God and the individual which has already been signed and sealed in this life. It will not be on the basis of any merit, 'for all have sinned and fall short of the glory of God' (Rom. 3:23). The next verse explains how it is possible for a righteous God to pronounce a 'Not Guilty' verdict over those who actually were guilty, but have repented in this life (apologised to God and turned away from their sins of thought, word and deed; of omission and commission). Such people 'are justified freely by his grace through the redemption that came by Christ Jesus'. In fact, a penalty *was* paid – by God himself on our behalf, through the sin-bearing death of his Son on the cross. That is the wonder of the gospel: the good news of Christianity. All who put their trust in Christ, who died for them, are set free from the condemnation of sin. Salvation is a free gift to believers, but it cost God dear.

It is vital to be clear that there is only one way to be granted eternal life – to be 'in Christ', who is the way, the truth and the life. He does not just point out the way, nor preach the truth, nor speak words of life – he embodies all three. In him is life: the life of God. Those who are 'in him' share eternal life; outside of him there is no eternal life, because to be outside of Christ is to be outside of God, and therefore of divine life (John 10:30; 11:25–6). No merit of any human being can save; no good works are good enough; even martyrdom is not in itself a qualification. No religious system, whether Christian or otherwise, provides the solution; even the Bible itself cannot save. Jesus once told Jewish religious leaders: 'You diligently study the Scriptures because you think that by them you possess eternal life. These are the Scriptures that testify about me, yet you refuse to come to me to have life' (John 5:39–40).

There is also only one way to be 'in Christ': by faith. This does not simply mean 'belief', but trust: the kind of trust which recognises the inability of any human being to achieve reconciliation with God; which abandons self to God's way of salvation; which results in dedication, by the power of God the Holy Spirit, to live for God in gratitude and love, by serving others and so extending his kingdom.

Those who have never heard

What of the millions who had, or have, no knowledge of Jesus? There is in fact clear New Testament teaching about this vital subject, in the first few chapters of the letter to the Romans. It is missed by many who study them, because they tend to concentrate on their main thrust, which is to show that Jew and Gentile alike have sinned, by falling short of God's standards, and need a Saviour. But in making out a watertight case for this, St Paul also shows that Jews and Gentiles who lived before Christ, who *believed* in the revelation of God through creation, conscience or the law, rather than relying on merit, were accepted by God. The example given is of Abraham, who 'believed God, and it was credited to him as righteousness' (Rom. 4:3). Paul stresses that Abraham believed before he was circumcised, i.e. before he became the founder member of the Jewish race. He is therefore the father of all who believe, both Jew and Gentile. When we consider how little Abraham could have known about God at that time (before all the revelation available to us in Scripture), it provides enormous hope that there have been millions of people throughout history who may have taken the same path of faith in the Creator God. God's Son had to become incarnate at a particular time in history, but the cross of Christ spans the whole of time. God is well able to apply its benefits retrospectively.

If there is such clear hope of salvation for Jews and Gentiles who trusted in the one, true Creator God, according to the light they had received *before* the time of Christ, what of those *after* the time of Christ, who have never heard the gospel? The authors believe that where it is not possible for a person to 'hear the gospel' (that can happen in all kinds of ways, some far less obvious than others), God treats them in the same way as those prior to the time of Christ. This could apply to whole nations before the gospel was taken to their shores; or to ethnic, tribal or language groups which have never heard; or to those prevented by their upbringing in a closed cultural or religious group from being able to discover the truth for themselves; or to very young children or mentally handicapped people, who are unable to understand the gospel in any generally recognised sense. If God could have mercy not only on Abraham, but on a tribal priest-king, Melchizedek (who was a Gentile described in Genesis chapter 14 as priest of God Most High, considered worthy even to bless Abraham two thousand years before Christ), it is but a small thing for him to draw out embryonic faith in himself as Creator God from individuals across the globe in their hundreds of thousands, stretching back in time and forward into the future. Where there is genuine faith in response to revelation which is from God, as opposed to man-made religious systems, then God has mercy.

We read in the Epistle to the Romans that 'since the creation of the world God's invisible qualities – his eternal power and divine nature – have been clearly seen, being understood from what has been made, so that men are without excuse' (Rom. 1:20). The key to salvation is faith in revelation. Just faith on its own will not do, because anyone could invent a religion – and many do. It must be God-given faith in God-given revelation of the one, true Creator God. The means of salvation, vital to achieve reconciliation with God, is the Christ-event. Where this may be known, God expects people to seek until they find. Where that knowledge, for one reason or another (not, of course, apathy or laziness) is genuinely not accessible, then God treats individuals, we believe, as he treated those before the time of Christ. All true believers are saved through Jesus Christ – but not all are *fully* aware of *how* they are saved.

Rewards for believers

Although God welcomes into heaven all who are 'in Christ', there is clear teaching in various passages of Scripture about differences of reward in the next life. Here is an example:

> Then Jesus said to his disciples, 'If anyone would come after me, he must deny himself and take up his cross and follow me. For whoever wants to save his life will lose it, but whoever loses his life for me will find it. What good will it be for a man if he gains the whole world, yet forfeits his soul? Or what can a man give in exchange for his soul? For the Son of Man is going to come in his Father's glory with his angels, and then he will reward each person according to what he has done.' (Matt. 16:24–7)

This can sound strange to our ears, particularly when we have grasped that we are not accepted by God on the basis of any merit of our own, but because of what Jesus has done for us; and that we should serve God, not with any thought of reward, but out of self-sacrificial love. It almost seems to detract from that to read about rewards in the next life. But God would fail to be just if he treated every Christian in the same way. We are saved by faith, but judged by 'works' (all that we have thought, said or done; our character, life and service for God). Even though (as we shall see in the next section) a process of purification takes place for believers on the Day of Judgment, that only removes remaining sin. God will still differentiate between one believer and the next, with absolute fairness, so ensuring that a Christian who has spent a lifetime serving God and other people with selfless motives is not treated in the same way as someone who has wasted God-given talents.

The clearest teaching about rewards is in the parable of the talents (Luke 19:11–26), in which Jesus stresses that each person has been given various gifts (some few, some many), and is answerable to God for the way in which they are used. (The parable in Matthew 20:1–16, about the labourer who arrived at the eleventh hour and was given the same wage as one early on the scene, is not a contradiction of this teaching, because in the second parable it seems that circumstances rather than laziness prevented an earlier arrival.) Teaching on rewards, whether given by Jesus or the apostles, was not intended as a kind of bribe, because it is usually linked with an emphasis on self-denial, and the reward is not material but related to getting to know God better. But the teaching about rewards is partly prophetic, as there are hints elsewhere in Scripture suggesting that rewards are also connected with roles in the next life, based on the way individuals have lived out their faith in this life.

Sadly, most Christians are so ill-informed about the next life, or regard it as so remote, that they rarely give serious thought to how they will actually spend eternity. But there are strong hints in the Bible (e.g. in 1 Cor. 6:2–3) that the saints (the biblical term for all believers, not just exceptional Christians) will share Christ's rule, exercising authority in varying positions of influence. To coin a phrase, we are in training for reigning. In Revelation 3:21 we read: 'To him who overcomes, I will give the right to sit with me on my throne, just as I overcame and sat down with my Father on his throne.' One can only surmise that life in heaven on earth will be organised through delegation to the saints, who will be allocated greater or lesser roles, much as appears to be the case in the angelic realm. There will be no room for envy, because the allocation of roles will be seen to be completely just.

Judgment of believers

Although those who trust God are saved by faith, they are still judged 'by works'. In other words, although God grants them eternal life with him, any sin still unrepented at the end of their lives will be scrutinised and purified. That is because it is recognised in the New Testament that repentance in this life is likely to be imperfect and partial. In particular, many believers may be unaware of impure motives in their way of life or ministry. Such impurities cannot be allowed to contaminate heaven. St Paul, using vivid imagery, writes of the contrast between building upon the basis of initial faith in Christ, either with that which counts for eternity, or with what proves to be rubbish under the scrutiny of Christ the Judge. This distinction will be revealed on Judgment Day, leading to a process of purification. He describes it like this:

> For no one can lay any foundation other than the one already laid, which is Jesus Christ. If any man builds on this foundation using gold, silver, costly stones, wood, hay or straw, his work will be shown for what it is, because the Day will bring it to light. It will be revealed with fire, and the fire will test the quality of each man's work. If what he has built survives, he will receive his reward. If it is burned up, he will suffer loss; he himself will be saved, but only as one escaping through the flames. (1 Cor. 3:11–15)

This passage of Scripture is not a basis for belief in Purgatory – if by that is meant a time of purification between death and the Second Coming, which leaves open the possibility that even those who have ignored or rejected Christ in this life could be transformed, particularly through the prayers of the saints. Rather, the parable Jesus told of the rich man and Lazarus makes it clear that eternal destiny is settled in this life (Luke 16:19–31). However, there would seem to be a (possibly brief) time of purification of *believers* on the great Day of Judgment. We are furnished with no further details as to what is meant, but one way of picturing it might be that each believer is granted understanding of *God's* view of his or her life and ministry at different stages, with searing revelations about motives, heart attitudes, lack of faith, missed opportunities to love and serve God and others, together with any remaining unconfessed sin of more obvious nature. (But nothing, however terrible, which has already been confessed in this life will be dredged up again. God's forgiveness is complete – he removes our sins 'as far as the east is from the west', as we read in Psalm 103:12.) There will then be some kind of purification process, when perhaps we are filled with regret, even anguish, to realise what we might have accomplished for our Lord in this life, if only we had trusted him more, lived a more wholehearted life of service and sought the daily empowering of the Holy Spirit. Only after this process will it be possible to begin life in heaven on earth, experiencing the presence of the holy God continuously, with all sin, failure and anguish about shortcomings consigned to history.

Lost without Christ

It has been right to emphasise God's primary purpose of salvation; to show that the category of those who are 'in Christ' could be far broader than many Christians appreciate; and to explain the process of purification which believers face at the time of Judgment Day. But the nagging question will not go away: what is the fate of those who are outside of Christ? This category includes all who have chosen to reject or ignore God's way of salvation through his Son; all who could have made an effort to discover the key to eternal life (faith in Christ), but did not get round to it; all who have chosen a life of sin, whether blatant crime, wrongdoing or secret sin; all who have lived for self, ignoring God who made them, and the needs of others whom they could have helped; all who have oppressed other human beings; all who thought they were religious, but failed to understand that love is at the heart of true faith; all who claimed to be Christian, but mistook formulas for a personal relationship with Jesus Christ; all who, if they genuinely had no opportunity to hear the gospel, did not respond to the revelation of the one, true Creator God, the knowledge of whom is available to every human being who has ever lived. Anyone in those categories, among others, who truly repents in this life, turning away from the past and trusting God for the future, will be forgiven. Even last-minute repentance is enough, as we learn from the story of the thief on the cross. It would be dangerous, though, to presume that there will be an opportunity to turn to God at the eleventh hour: nobody knows how suddenly death might come. There is no hint in the Bible of any second chance for salvation after death – just the opposite. 'Man is destined to die once, and after that to face judgment' (Heb. 9:27). In the end, only those whom God the Father recognises as being 'in Christ' will be saved from condemnation.

Christ as the Judge

In John 5:21–3 we read:

> For just as the Father raises the dead and gives them life, even so the Son gives life to whom he is pleased to give it. Moreover, the Father judges no one, but has entrusted all judgment to the Son, that all may honour the Son just as they honour the Father. He who does not honour the Son does not honour the Father, who sent him.

This truth, that Jesus himself is the Judge on that awesome day of final judgment for humanity, is the key to the basis on which we shall be judged. After all, this same Jesus loved humanity so much that he gave his own life to die for the sins of the world. Does that mean that he will be soft on sin? That is to miss the point, because elsewhere we read: 'God has given us eternal life, and this life is in his Son. He who has the Son has life; he who does not have the Son of God does not have life' (1 John 5:11–12). Jesus himself will instantly recognise those who are indwelt by his life through the Holy Spirit, and only they will be ushered into God's presence. The rest are unable to experience that, because they have chosen, whether deliberately or by default, to remove themselves from the source of eternal life in Christ.

The 'Guilty' verdict is pronounced on the basis of lack of faith in God through Christ. But the *sentence* will differ from person to person, according to the way of life of each individual. Another, perhaps rather too simplistic, way of putting this is that the verdict of 'Guilty' or 'Not Guilty' is pronounced according to one's attitude to God in this life, but the sentence is passed according to one's attitude to other human beings. It will be seen at the time to be completely just and utterly appropriate, matching the nature of the way of life of each individual. The person who has lived a fairly decent life, even an altruistic one, but ignored God, will surely not be treated in the same way as someone guilty of obvious wrongdoing. Then again, there will be obvious differences in sentence between someone who, for instance, has behaved in unloving ways towards family members, and a person who has committed crimes against humanity.

Views of hell

More needs to be said about the sentence meted out, but first we need to look at different ideas about hell. The traditional popular view was of everlasting punishment for the damned, who would suffer literal torment, including of a physical nature, but in varying degrees. So Shakespeare's King Lear exclaimed: 'Beneath is all the fiend's: there's hell, there's darkness, there is the sulphurous pit, burning, scalding, stench, consumption; fie, fie, fie!'

Other writers who believe in a literal hell have interpreted lurid biblical language as descriptions of mental torment, varying from perpetual anguish in the tortured soul of a person who has inflicted pain on others, to the deep regret of someone who has denied the existence of God, only to discover his reality when it is too late.

Some theologians believe in universalism, partly because they are convinced that a loving God would not allow anyone ultimately to spend eternity without him. They believe that everyone will get to heaven in the end, as Christ continues his work of reconciliation. This position not only ignores justice, but also means that God forces those who have ignored or rejected his Son to commit themselves to a relationship with him. This is the opposite of the way God works, which is to allow human beings to decide whether or not to worship him in love.

Other scholars, including some who regard the Bible as authoritative, have in recent decades favoured annihilationism – the view that God decrees on Judgment Day that those in Christ have eternal life, but those outside of Christ cease to exist. This is called conditional immortality. They base this mainly on analysis of biblical words related to destruction, which can be interpreted as absolute extinction, and the phrase 'the second death', which is used in Revelation 20:14. The major problem with this view is that all unbelievers would be treated alike, regardless of whether they have perpetrated massive crimes against humanity or refused to forgive one other person. Other scholars have conjectured that, rather than suffering an everlasting sentence, there are differences of degree in feelings of remorse which people experience when face to face with a holy God. Perhaps their lives are 'played back' to them, showing the different choices which could have been made. Those latter views are, of course, supposition, but if held together with the view of ultimate annihilation sound more reasonable to modern ears than taking everlasting torment literally. But does this view really do justice to justice?

We would prefer to stress the necessity for the absolute justice of God to be seen to be done, which will be shown by his passing widely differing sentences. These will be recognised as completely just by the individuals concerned. They will exactly relate to the beliefs and way of life on this earth chosen by those outside of Christ. It is not possible for us to imagine what these sentences will be. Very often, God allows people to have their own way. There is likely to be an obvious element of abandoning people to the consequences of the choices they have made. It could be that annihilation takes place after varying periods of time, when justice has been done. As for where the sentences will be carried out, the authors agree to disagree on the next point of view! It is based on a passage from 2 Peter chapter 3 (italics ours):

> Long ago by God's word the heavens existed and the earth was formed . . . By the same word the present heavens and earth are reserved for fire, being kept *for* the day of judgment and destruction of ungodly men . . . But the day of the Lord will come like a thief. The heavens will disappear with a roar; the elements will be destroyed by fire, and the earth and everything in it will be laid bare . . . But in keeping with his promise we are looking forward to a new heaven and a new earth, the home of righteousness. (2 Pet. 3:5, 7, 10, 13)

The word in italics translated 'for' could mean 'until', or 'for the purpose of'. Therefore, one interpretation of these verses could be that the future of the ungodly is bound up with the future of planet Earth and its ultimate destruction. A number of scriptures refer to the ungodly being 'left', when the godly are caught up in the air to meet the returning Jesus. It is possible that after Judgment Day, those without Christ continue to live on this planet, possibly only for a short time. There could be vast variation in the quality of their existence, while they face up to their choices in this life. God will turn his face from them, much to their deep and lasting regret, but will continue to exercise his sovereign authority as to what happens to each person, as his sentences are carried out. These might vary perhaps, from his dealings with a humanitarian atheist, who may be permitted for a while an existence which is bearable, yet filled with regret at having denied God, to a cruel oppressor possibly feeling within himself all the agony of those he has harmed. Their sentence is everlasting in that it continues as long as the earth, with its space–time dimension. Then God (whether sooner or later) speaks the word which destroys the earth and all who inhabit it – perhaps in a moment of time. This view therefore incorporates annihilation, but after justice has been seen to be done. It also takes literally the word 'everlasting' but interprets it for the ungodly as meaning 'as long as time on the earth lasts', but for the godly as meaning 'for all eternity'. No one can presume on immortality – it is conditional. Only God is inherently immortal.

The main argument against this view would be from those who think it unacceptable that this earth will be totally destroyed, or reserved for such a terrible purpose. They believe renewal and restoration to be more consistent with the ways of God. Yet it is possible to take the interpretation of 2 Peter 3 above and still hold the view that after the destruction of the earth, whether partial or almost total, God takes what is left as the starting point for the new earth. It is therefore possible to believe in an initial hell on earth, followed by its destruction, followed by heaven on earth (either a renewed or totally new planet). Meanwhile, it seems that the saints are somehow involved in administering God's justice (1 Cor. 6:2–3).

Some problems resolved

This view, of a temporal hell on the old earth replaced by heaven on the new, renewed earth, solves a number of problems. It is difficult otherwise to answer the question: where is hell? The world view of biblical writers, perpetuated into the middle ages, was that hell was 'down below'. This simplistic view has long been abandoned, to be replaced by some regarding it as in a different dimension, which will be invisible to the godly; others even believe God has chosen another planet for the purpose. The temporal (as well as the 'everlasting') view of hell also provides a reason for an actual resurrection of the ungodly, which is taught in Scripture. (Even so, it is difficult to think that God would clothe the ungodly in glorious bodies, as he will the godly, only for these people then to suffer judgment of some kind. The difference between the bodily state of believers and unbelievers is not spelt out in the Bible, but one can only imagine that the latter will be more akin to resuscitation, rather than resurrection.) As for ultimate annihilation, God has the power to destroy matter without trace if he chooses (unlike human beings who can only change it by chemical processes, or convert it into energy). God only needs to speak the word to destroy utterly not only the bodies but also the spirits of the ungodly. The view of annihilation after possibly a brief time of judgment satisfies the desire for justice, without the need to think of the ungodly suffering for all eternity. If there is a sense of passage of time after death, the thought of people enduring God's wrath, literally for ever and ever, would seem abhorrent by any reckoning. Further confirmation of the view of a temporal hell might be found in Revelation chapter 20, where we read, after a description of the Last Judgment, that death and Hades were thrown into the lake of fire (verse 14). But when all has been said, nobody will really know the truth of these matters until the next life.

Judgment and forgiveness

Jesus exhorted his disciples to forgive those who had offended them 'seventy-seven times'. He taught us to pray 'Forgive us our sins, as we forgive those who sin against us'. Although we have seen that God cannot let people off without justice being done, it seems at first sight inconsistent with Jesus' teaching that, after perhaps a sentence has been served or even a cry of remorse uttered on Judgment Day, God does not forgive the ungodly. That is because there is a vast difference between an absolutely holy God in his dealings with humankind and the way in which people should treat one another. All human beings are imperfect. The ideal is that if there has been an offence, there is repentance, forgiveness and, if necessary, restitution. Where there is no repentance, we should still have an attitude of forgiveness, even though there will be an incompleteness about that situation. Human forgiveness is an acknowledgment that we all fail in different ways, and want to reflect God's forgiveness which is available through Christ. But there is no imperfection in the nature of God, nor can any be allowed in his presence. His absolute justice demands appropriate penalties. Where there is repentance in this life, he forgives completely, but only because his Son has paid the ultimate penalty for all sin. Where there is no repentance in this life – in other words an acknowledgment of wrongdoing, an acceptance by faith of Jesus' mediation between God and man, and a desire to turn away from that behaviour – then there can be no forgiveness. We have seen that even those who have repented, and placed their trust in God's Son for eternal life, still have to go through a time of purification before being welcomed into heaven. If God were to forgive lightly, that would be to undermine the depth of what Jesus did in laying down his life for the sins of the world. It would undermine God's holiness. It would undermine absolute justice. It would undermine the perfection of heaven.

Depart from me

Those are the terrible words which God will utter to many people on Judgment Day. Although consideration of hell is an appalling subject, it is all too easy to become involved in theoretical debate. It is also possible through human sympathy (which by contrast with true divine compassion can easily mislead us) to avoid the subject, or even dismiss the concept. We need to be reminded that, according to the word of God, one day it will become reality for millions. This will only sink into our minds if we understand how terrible it is to ignore or reject the God of the whole universe and his revealed plan of salvation – the ultimate in self-giving love. It is also a dreadful matter to treat people created in the image of God with anything but sacrificial love, in thought, word and deed. Anything less than that – let alone disrespect, contempt, cruelty, unspeakable deeds – deserves hell. Although shocked by the concept of hell, we should also be overwhelmed by the knowledge that God took the initiative to plan salvation through Jesus, to rescue us from hell and to welcome us into his presence in heaven. Throughout this life, the Holy Spirit offers eternal life to all who are willing to receive it.

Incentive to witness

In the light of this knowledge Christians should sense an *urgency* to share Jesus with others. The overriding motivation will be love – a longing for relatives and friends to 'grasp how wide and long and high and deep is the love of Christ, and to know this love that surpasses knowledge' (Eph. 3:18–19). No special techniques are required – just a willingness to seize the right opportunity to share personal experience of a relationship with Jesus, based on some of the promises of God in the Bible. More often, actions speak louder than words. Ministering to those in need, whether caring for a sick relative or alleviating suffering on a bigger scale, is an imperative for every follower of the One who had compassion on the crowds. Such ministry should be carried out in love, because each individual is made in the image of God. Jesus healed all who came to him – he did not discriminate, nor did he minister only to those he knew would respond to his message. It is, of course, a wonderful bonus when someone does! Awareness that all human beings will one day stand before God, only to face banishment from his presence if they are not in Christ, should give a cutting edge to evangelism. It may not necessarily be part of the initial message conveyed, but it certainly should remove complacency in the messenger.

Chapter 4

Will Jesus ever return?

'This same Jesus, who has been taken from you into heaven, will come back in the same way you have seen him go into heaven.'

(Acts 1:11)

Two comings

Two things are certain: the Second Coming of Jesus to planet Earth will be totally different from the first coming; and when it does take place it will transcend all expectations. The Person who comes is the same: the one and only Jesus Christ, the Son of God; but there could be no greater contrast than between the manner of his two advents (comings) to the earth. The first took place in a way that was hidden from all but a few. Mary and Joseph were the only people present, as far as we know. Since St Luke informs us that Mary placed her new-born baby in a manger, it would seem that Jesus' birth took place in a stable, of all places, perhaps observed by a few animals. A heavenly choir alerted a handful of shepherds, while wise men from the East arrived later, after following a guiding star. This story has been so world-renowned for two thousand years that we cease to be amazed that God the Father actually planned that God the Son, who had existed from all eternity, should become man in such a humble context. In fact, all the circumstances surrounding the birth and life of Jesus were so unlike the expectations of the religious scholars of the time that few of them came to recognise that he was the Christ (or Messiah), foretold by their prophets. The two people who were the most discerning were an elderly man and a widow who was eighty-four years old. They saw no star to guide them, nor were they privileged to hear angelic voices. Their story is told in the second chapter of Luke's gospel, in the context of Jesus being presented in the temple when he was eight days old. It seems that both these old people were so open to the prompting of the Holy Spirit that they realised as soon as they saw the infant Jesus that this was 'the Lord's Christ' (Luke 2:26).

A sobering lesson

Every Christmas, prophecies from the Old Testament are read in church services. These were some of the many clues which the Holy Spirit provided for the Jewish people, that God's chosen deliverer would come. But if it were possible for us to study them without the benefit of hindsight, it is likely that our expectations would have tallied with the prevailing views of the time. The Jews believed that a descendant would be born in the line of King David who would exceed him in greatness, overthrow the occupying forces of the Jewish territory and establish an empire which would outshine even that of David's son, Solomon. There would follow a time without end of peace and prosperity for God's chosen people. Those prophecies of Scripture which we now realise revealed a totally different perspective (such as the 'Suffering Servant' passages in Isaiah) were thought by some to refer to the travail of the Jewish race prior to these events. Little wonder that only a minority of Jewish people ever recognised that not only were all the prophecies taken together fulfilled in Jesus, but that the whole of the Old Testament – its laws, prescribed rituals and historical accounts – pointed to him.

If only Christians would learn humility from this object lesson. Instead, many Protestant groups in particular have formed such definite (but often widely divergent) views on the Second Coming, that some have even separated off to form a new denomination on the basis of a particular interpretation.

Extremist sects have camped out on mountain-tops, convinced that 'the end is nigh'- only to creep back down again, covered in confusion. Lurid books have been written about judgments, signs and a secret 'rapture' (snatching away) of the saints. Such controversies, and many more, have tended to bring this wonderful aspect of Christian teaching into disrepute. Although there is a renewal of interest in eschatology in academic circles, many preachers and teachers, other than perhaps in Pentecostal denominations, tend to avoid the subject, except for a brief mention on Advent Sunday. Afraid of heresy or extremism, or just daunted by what appears a complex subject, they prefer to concentrate on other aspects of doctrine, about which there is more general agreement among Christians who hold to traditional beliefs. Our hope is that this book will help to dispel some of those fears. On the basis of consultations we have previously held with Christian leaders who hold widely differing views, we eventually aim to demonstrate that there is more common ground than has previously been realised, when the subject is approached with humility.

A world-changing event

The basic biblical teaching on the return of Christ stresses, first, that 'this same Jesus' (Acts 1:11) will definitely come back to the earth (which is astonishing in itself), and second, that it will be a dramatic event, paving the way for the end of the world as we know it. The various accounts are remarkably consistent. The message is: Jesus, who ascended after his resurrection, disappearing in the clouds, will 'come down from heaven, with a loud command, with the voice of the archangel and with the trumpet call of God' (1 Thess. 4:16). This is the signal for the resurrection of those who have died 'in Christ', followed by the ascension and bodily transformation of believers who are alive at the time. According to the prophecies of Jesus himself, this is the time of separation from unbelievers, who are left behind. His return will be preceded by various 'signs', and will result in judgment of those who do not know God and do not obey the gospel of our Lord Jesus. They will be punished with everlasting destruction and shut out from the presence of the Lord and from the majesty of his power on the day he comes to be glorified in his holy people and to be marvelled at among all those who have believed (2 Thess. 1:8–10)

Once the separation has taken place between those 'in Christ' and those outside of Christ, there follows the purification of believers, the sentencing of unbelievers and, after destruction, the creation of the new heavens and earth. That would *seem* to be fairly clear from the prophecies of Jesus and Paul, even though totally awesome. However, certain other factors conspire to create a more complex picture.

A literal view?

If, as we have commented several times, biblical language about such matters as hell is not necessarily to be taken literally in every way, how could we ever substantiate a literal interpretation of scriptures to do with the Second Coming, for example? It is, after all, important to apply similar principles to New Testament scriptures on *all* 'end-time' (eschatological) matters: it would be subjective to pick and choose. In fact, we believe all the *concepts* (e.g. judgment, heaven, hell, the return of Jesus) refer to realities yet to be experienced, but the *details* are not to be taken literally. To put it another way: the subject matter of the picture being painted is of a real, rather than fictional (or even 'spiritualised') landscape, as yet future. But the details of the picture (the flames of hell, the precious stones of heaven, the sound of the trumpet heralding Jesus' return) point to aspects which transcend not only human experience, but even human imagination. The writers had to find ways of describing the indescribable. Those who are unable to comprehend this could make a similar mistake to Jewish religious leaders of the first century, who had developed their views along such detailed lines that they were unprepared for the prophetic fulfilment which God had planned.

Some scholars reinterpret end-time concepts in Scripture,

believing that they refer to this age, but the most important argument against those views is that Christianity is incomplete without a glorious future becoming reality, not only for individuals but for redeemed humanity. Wonderful though it is to be able to enjoy a relationship with God here and now; important though it is to work and pray for God's will to be done on earth as in heaven (including improvements in the lot of suffering humanity), it is obvious that any results in line with God's purposes can only ever be imperfect, partial and provisional in this world. Before the two world wars, some Christian scholars thought God's kingdom would come on earth through a moral and spiritual evolutionary process, by which the world would gradually be more christianised in beliefs and morals. Their disillusionment is not difficult to imagine. Nothing short of a dramatic manifestation of the lordship of Christ to the whole earth could usher in the ultimate fulfilment of God's purpose: the reconciliation of the entire universe in Christ. Only when Jesus returns will evil be destroyed, leading to God's sole reign over creation, nations and all human beings. Only then will the new creation of the heavens, the earth and human bodies be possible. History is moving inexorably to that climax, which will be so glorious that no words – apocalyptic, mystical or prosaic – could ever describe it: 'No eye has seen, no ear has heard, no mind has conceived what God has prepared for those who love him' (1 Cor. 2:9).

Characteristics of prophecy

There are several important clues which help to interpret biblical prophecy.

The first is the *multiple reference* of some predictions. Many prophecies have more than one fulfilment, or to be more accurate, have one or more partial fulfilments before pointing to an ultimate and complete realisation. An obvious example of this is the prophecy in Joel chapter 2, which partially came to pass on the Day of Pentecost, when all the disciples were filled with the Holy Spirit (Acts 2:1–21). There have been other spectacular outpourings of the Holy Spirit on groups of people since then (as well as a fulfilment every time an individual becomes a Christian, which can only happen through the Spirit). But certain aspects of that prophecy have not yet been fulfilled.

There is also the *concertina* effect. When observed from a vantage point, a mountain range can appear like continuous undulating land. The observer may not be standing sufficiently far above other peaks to appreciate the deep valleys in between the various mountain-tops. So one prophecy may refer to several events, sometimes separated by vast periods of time. This separation and time-lapse were sometimes hidden even from the prophet, and the unwary reader may not always notice the valleys, either. There are numerous examples of this, including many Old Testament prophecies which initially refer, for instance, to the return from exile, but move on to speak of the age of the Spirit, inaugurated by Jesus (e.g. Jeremiah 31). It is impossible to know just how much the prophets understood about the actual meaning of their messages. In some cases, such as Isaiah 53, which was first interpreted by Philip the apostle as referring to the death of Jesus (Acts 8:32–5), it is highly likely that the prophet had no idea that his words referred to the suffering and death of the Son of God.

Sometimes contrasting prophecies (our name for them is *dual-aspect*) are given about the same event, to draw out different aspects. This has led some to interpret them mistakenly as referring to two separate events. The two descriptions of the Second Coming in 1 Thessalonians 4 and 2 Thessalonians 1–2 have been thought by some to refer to two separate comings of Christ: one for the resurrection of the saints, and the other for the punishment of the ungodly. It is far more likely that they refer to very different results for believers and unbelievers of the one coming.

Finally in this section, prophecy is not just, or even mainly, predictive. It is *purposive*. (The technical term for that is 'teleological'.) It includes foretelling only in the context of forthtelling, which means speaking out God's word of encouragement, challenge or warning to the immediate audience or readership (but very often including a message of timeless significance). This is the main characteristic of biblical prophecy, compared with predictions by fortune-tellers, which only serve either to raise superficial hopes of love, fame or fortune, etc., or to bring people into fear. Sometimes disasters have been predicted in this way, which have later come true, yet no possibility was provided of averting the accident. This is not the way of God. If he conveys glimpses of the future to his children, it is either to reveal the glorious completion of his purposes of salvation which have begun in the here and now, so giving incentive for deeper dedication, or to warn of difficult consequences *if* there is no repentance by (e.g.) an individual or church or nation. The only exception to this is when successive warnings have already been ignored, resulting in God making the final pronouncement of judgment. This happened, for instance, just before Jerusalem was conquered by the Babylonians in 586 BC. It also, of course, applies to the very last end-time events, when it is vital that evil is finally judged.

We shall apply these principles to teaching on the signs of Jesus' return, but first look at an aspect which perplexes many Christians.

A secret rapture?

Many popular books have been written about this view, which is widely held, especially in Christian fundamentalist circles in the USA. In 1 Thessalonians 4:16–17 we read that, when the Lord returns, 'the dead in Christ will rise first. After that, we who are still alive and are left will be caught up together with them in the clouds to meet the Lord in the air.' The words 'caught up' have been translated 'raptured' in the past, from the Latin *rapere*, which means 'to seize' or 'to snatch'. The view of the secret rapture is that, when Jesus returns, believers will be secretly whisked away from the trials of the last 'Great Tribulation'. It is also based on the many scriptures which warn believers to be ready, for Jesus will return at a time when he is least expected. In particular it makes much of Luke 17:20–35:

> Once, having been asked by the Pharisees when the kingdom of God would come, Jesus replied, 'The kingdom of God does

not come with your careful observation, nor will people say, "Here it is," or "There it is," because the kingdom of God is within you.' Then he said to his disciples, 'The time is coming when you will long to see one of the days of the Son of Man, but you will not see it. Men will tell you, "There he is!" or "Here he is!" Do not go running off after them. For the Son of Man in his day will be like the lightning, which flashes and lights up the sky from one end to the other. But first he must suffer many things and be rejected by this generation. Just as it was in the days of Noah, so also will it be in the days of the Son of Man. People were eating, drinking, marrying and being given in marriage up to the day Noah entered the ark. Then the flood came and destroyed them all . . . It will be just like this on the day the Son of Man is revealed. On that day no one who is on the roof of his house, with his goods inside, should go down to get them. Likewise, no one in the field should go back for anything . . . I tell you, on that night two people will be in one bed; one will be taken and the other left. Two women will be grinding grain together; one will be taken and the other left.'

The account in this chapter majors on the suddenness of Jesus' return, compared with the account in Luke chapter 21, which emphasises signs. In fact, the first three verses quoted appear to warn against looking for signs. In addition, 1 Thessalonians 4 stresses that Jesus is coming back for believers, whereas 2 Thessalonians 1–2 emphasises judgment on unbelievers. In the light of these differences, the view of the secret rapture has been propounded. The main points made are:

1   Jesus' Second Coming will be dramatic and visible to believers but secret and invisible from the rest of humanity. They will be left behind, only for Jesus to return a third time in judgment.
2   The Second Coming could take place at any time, without any signs, but the third will be preceded by signs, which will take the shape of terrible judgments on earth.
3   Therefore, when the secret rapture occurs, there would

initially be complete bewilderment that millions of people have suddenly disappeared!

We could not endorse this view, but rather regard it as a misunderstanding of biblical paradox. Just as different Old Testament prophecies about the Messiah seemed contradictory – some pointing to a great deliverer, some to a suffering servant – but in fact were two sides of the same coin, so we believe that to be the case with some New Testament prophecies. There will be one dramatic return of Christ – glorious for believers, terrible for unbelievers. A surprise to the former, even those who are to some extent prepared; a dreadful shock to the latter. It also seems difficult to believe that the Second Coming could take place secretly, or that God would leave the world without the witness of the Church, at its time of greatest need. Despite our differences with those who hold this view, we understand how they came to believe it, and respect their integrity.

Signs of the Second Coming?

Many New Testament prophecies about Jesus' return are preceded by dire warnings of calamities on earth. As a result many readers reason that believers should be on the alert to compare contemporary events with Scripture, noticing 'the signs of the times' so that the Second Coming is not a total shock. On the face of it, this view seems to have been brought into disrepute, because down through the centuries it has led to successive generations of Christians believing that this climactic event was certain to take place in their lifetime. As a result, much scholarly research has taken place, either to show that the prophecies of Jesus and those in the book of Revelation (which we shall look at in a later chapter) were all fulfilled in the first century AD, or to try to think of the signs in a different way. But if we bear in mind the characteristics of prophecy mentioned above, it should be possible to resolve the apparent confusion. Most important is that the Holy Spirit inspired the prophecies of Jesus and the apostles for a purpose: he *intended* that each generation should be on the alert for the return of

Jesus. To put it simply: he planned a certain ambiguity, to prevent the Church becoming too complacent at any stage in its history. Believers are urged to watch and pray, to examine their lives, to engage in mission, to care for the needy, to use their talents – in case the Master returns and they are found to have failed him.

The prophecies of Jesus about the 'signs' (in Matthew 24, Mark 13 and Luke 21) were given when the disciples asked him a specific question: 'when will this happen [i.e. the overthrow of the temple], and what will be the sign of your coming and of the end of the age?' (Matt. 24:3) The lengthy answer, including earthquakes, wars and persecution, may be interpreted as having been fulfilled in one sense, leading up to the destruction of Jerusalem, but also seems to have further reference to end-time events, as one would expect from the question asked. Even though this appears to be a specific answer to a specific question, many scholars insist that Jesus never intended his followers to regard his reply as indicating a series of events to take place, after which he would return. But to begin with, we shall look at a list of these signs. After that we shall show that there seems to have been both a preliminary fulfilment and intermediate fulfilments, and we shall look at a possible final realisation.

The signs outlined by Jesus

- False christs and false alarms about a second advent
- Wars and rumours of wars
- Revolutions
- Famines, earthquakes and pestilences
- Persecution of believers
- Widespread apostasy
- False prophets performing counterfeit miracles to deceive, if possible, the elect
- Increase in wickedness
- Jerusalem trampled on by the Gentiles, *until* the time of the Gentiles is fulfilled
- The gospel preached throughout the world as a testimony to the nations (after which the end will come)

- The abomination that causes desolation will desecrate the holy place
- Signs in the sun, moon, stars
- Signs on the earth (nations in perplexity at the roaring and tossing of the sea)
- Fearful events, a time of great distress (tribulation) unequalled in history, people fainting in terror, yet trying to continue 'normal' life. This period 'cut short' for the sake of the elect.

These signs are followed by the second advent of Christ, visible from East to West.

Historical fulfilments

There is no question that Jewish believers who lived through the terrible time when the Romans destroyed the second temple were convinced that all these prophecies were coming to pass there and then. There was a severe earthquake in Phrygia in AD 61, which did extensive damage; in AD 79 a fearful eruption of Vesuvius buried Pompeii; there were famines in the reigns of both Claudius and Nero; there were nearly always wars and rumours of wars on the borders of the Roman Empire; there was a terrible persecution of believers in the time of Nero, when it is likely that some forsook their faith although, by contrast, many Christians spread the gospel with even greater fervency throughout the Roman Empire; the Jewish rebellion against Rome, which led to the capture and destruction of Jerusalem, began in AD 66; Josephus wrote of a 'tailed star' which appeared over the doomed city for a considerable time; the actual siege of Jerusalem brought about appalling suffering; the temple was desecrated. In other words, virtually everything which Jesus predicted came to pass within forty years – except his return (the timing of which, he was at pains to point out, had not been revealed to him, although he did say the end would not come right away). It is also understandable that any Christians since that time who have endured famine, or been affected by natural disasters, or embroiled in war, or suffered persecution, or witnessed apostasy or spurious manifestations of spiritual power, have turned to these predictive words of Jesus. They would find comfort that he knows the end from the beginning, that he promises wisdom and strength in times of trial, that his Second Coming might well be soon. In particular, when one-third of the population of Western Christendom died from the Black Death in three years (1347–50) it does not take much imagination to understand why many were convinced that the end of the world was imminent. In the subsequent 650 years there have been many other false alarms.

Hazard lights?

In view of this, it becomes easier to appreciate the position of those who take the view that the signs are not to do with any understanding of when Jesus will return, but rather a warning that the conflict between good and evil will continue until he does. As Dr Stephen H. Travis wrote in *Christ Will Come Again* (Hodder and Stoughton, 1997):

> Why should we assume in our day we have got the equation right, when so many before us have been wrong? The signs of Mark 13 are not like the signs which say 'End of Motorway 1 mile'. They are in fact more like hazard warning lights which warn us of dangers along the way . . . of the conflict between . . . God's purpose and all that opposes it, which will go on until Christ finally defeats evil . . . the belief that the end of all things is due in the next few years . . . may stimulate evangelism, but it discourages people from proper planning and working towards a society which is more in harmony with God's will. (p. 123)

One has much sympathy with that view, in particular recognising how unhelpful it is if individuals, or groups of believers, are so taken up with trying to work out the signs of the times, even drawing up charts with precise details of what they believe will happen leading up to the Second Coming, that they neglect other aspects of Christian truth, or fail to work for the extension of the kingdom of God. We know personally of such cases, but we also know that some of the great social reformers of the last century held strong views about the return of Jesus (even to the extent that they worked for the return of the Jews to Palestine, believing that to be a sign which would hasten the advent of Christ).

More about signs

Despite the very real problem of false alarms, it seems inconceivable to us that God would not give some warnings and signs to the human race, when the world-shaking event of the return of his Son is about to happen! After all, this will mark the end of human history as we know it. God gave warnings through his prophets about the fall of Jerusalem and destruction of the temple, prior to the two occasions of 586 BC and AD 70. These judgments were definitive events in the history of his chosen people. He provided prophecies of the first advent. He also gave signs and warnings of less significant events. In his love, he will surely warn the human race of the approach of the end of this age, in particular giving final opportunities for repentance. Failure to do so would be totally inconsistent with the way God has worked throughout biblical history. Of course, there have been, and still are, dangers of getting the timing completely wrong, or overemphasising being on the alert to the detriment of working for God's kingdom here and now. That is the meaning of Jesus' warnings against sign-seeking. He particularly wanted to emphasise that the rule of God is not an external kingdom, but his lordship, especially within the human spirit. His warning was not against signs, but sign-*seeking* or getting too caught up in analysing signs. The fact that there are problems with signs does not mean they are not valid. Nearly all Christian truth is fraught with dangers of misunderstanding. God lives dangerously! He rarely spells out his truth with systematic clarity, but conveys it through hints, parables, stories, the complexity of human history, poetry and apparently mysterious prophecy.

It is true that the Greek word for 'signs' can mean warnings; another meaning is miracles. But in the context of the disciples asking Jesus what they could look for to indicate future events, including his return, it would seem that the more obvious (and common) meaning in Jesus' prophecies is signs of things to come. However, on closer examination of the prophecies given by Jesus in Luke 21, Mark 13 and Matthew 24, it becomes clearer that the signs fall into three categories. The first is of difficulties for believers, or more general disasters of various kinds, which were to recur down through the centuries (in more detail: false christs and false alarms about a second advent; wars and rumours of wars or revolutions; famines; earthquakes; plagues; persecution of believers). In respect to this category, we fully endorse the explanation given by Dr Stephen Travis, referred to above – namely, that Jesus was warning the disciples that very difficult events would take place throughout human history. The second category is of signs which herald the second advent: persecution of believers *by all nations*, including betrayal by lapsed believers or family members; widespread apostasy; false prophets performing counterfeit miracles which deceive, if that were possible, even 'the elect'; increase in wickedness; Jerusalem trampled on by the Gentiles *until* the time of the Gentiles is fulfilled (we shall look at this sign in a later chapter); the gospel preached throughout the world as a testimony to the nations (after which the end will come). We recognise that believers in the first two centuries could have thought these had been fulfilled, but since the whole world has only been discovered more recently, we now know that these signs have not yet had a final fulfilment, but are intended to herald the nearer approach of the Second Coming. The third category is of signs immediately preceding the Great Tribulation: a short time of terrible distress just before the Second Coming, unequalled in history, when people try to live a normal life, but are gripped by terror – there will be signs in the heavens; signs on the earth, including the roaring and tossing of the sea, which brings perplexity to nations; the abomination that causes desolation will desecrate the Holy Place (this will be discussed in Chapter 9).

Bearing in mind the characteristics of prophecy which have been mentioned, it is clear that most of them apply to the prophecies of Jesus. We have paid some attention to the concertina effect and multiple reference – how Jesus moves rapidly from talking about the destruction of the temple, to intermediate events, and beyond to his return. We have stressed the dual aspect, whereby the paradox of the Second Coming – its glory and terror – is conveyed by accounts stressing different aspects. We will show in the last chapter how the prophetic teaching of Jesus is purposive – emphasising holy living, spreading the gospel with urgency, trusting God in difficult circumstances, relying on the Holy Spirit for wisdom and strength in persecution, ministering to the needy, and looking forward in love to the return of the Bridegroom. We now look at the categories in more detail.

Recurring signs throughout history

This list of 'signs' recurring throughout history is easy to understand, but more difficult to comprehend is why they were mentioned at all, as such things as natural disasters are commonplace. In fact these are not true signs at all, strictly speaking, and a careful reading of Jesus' prophecies shows that he distinguishes between these on-going problems and the true signs nearer his return. This is clear particularly in the Matthew account (Matt. 24:3–9):

> As Jesus was sitting on the Mount of Olives, the disciples came to him privately. 'Tell us,' they said, 'when will this happen, and what will be the sign of your coming and of the end of the age?' Jesus answered: 'Watch out that no one deceives you. For many will come in my name, claiming, "I am the Christ," and will deceive many. You will hear of wars and rumours of wars, but see to it that you are not alarmed. Such things must happen, *but the end is still to come*. Nation will rise against nation, and kingdom against kingdom. There will be famines and earthquakes in various places. All these are the beginning of birth pains. Then . . . [Jesus proceeds to give further signs].

What is clear from these verses is that we should not have false expectations of a kind of utopia on earth, free of problems (whether freedom from persecution of Christians, or freedom from more general conflict caused by human sinfulness, or freedom from natural disasters) this side of the Second Coming. That is important to bear in mind, given extravagant claims made by a minority of Christians about miraculous by-products of a longed-for world-wide revival of Christianity.

Some, on the other hand, have claimed that one sign of the return of Jesus would be an escalation of natural disasters beforehand. It would be difficult to find support for that claim in these chapters, but it is one interpretation of passages in Revelation. If that proves to be the case, it may well be due mainly to population increase, which inevitably means that more people have to live in hazardous places. For example, 250,000 perished in China in 1976, in the worst ever earthquake in history in terms of the number of lives lost – the consequence of the epicentre being directly beneath a densely populated city. The worst loss of life ever in a natural disaster occurred in Bangladesh in 1970, where people live in crowded conditions in areas known to be vulnerable to cyclones and subsequent flooding. On that occasion, 300,000 people lost their lives immediately, and up to a million died within months from diseases linked with the polluted flood-water.

We now move on to the second list of signs, leaving the third category, which is linked with the Great Tribulation, until the chapter on Revelation.

Signs that Christ is soon to return

Then you will be handed over to be persecuted and put to death, and you will be hated by all nations because of me. At that time many will turn away from the faith and will betray and hate each other, and many false prophets will appear and deceive many people. Because of the increase of wickedness, the love of most will grow cold, but he who stands firm to the end will be saved. And this gospel of the kingdom will be preached in the whole world as a testimony to all nations, and then the end will come. (Matt. 24:9–14)

These, we believe, are signs in the sense of real events in future history providing warning and encouragement that Jesus' return is at hand. Their common characteristic is that they refer to world-wide developments, the first being world-wide evangelism. In bygone centuries, understanding of the true extent of the nations of the world was inevitably limited. Some early Christians, thinking the Roman Empire was the entire inhabited world, made claims, which they believed to be true, that the gospel had been taken to all the world within a remarkably short space of time. But others would have been aware of 'uncivilised' peoples beyond the Roman borders, or of the 'silk route' to the East, where traders knew that different empires held sway. Obviously, the true world-wide missionary movement only began when explorers discovered the full extent of the continents and islands, and even today there remain a number of tribal groups as yet unreached with the gospel. Modern travel and communications have enormously accelerated the possibilities of world evangelisation, such that the true fulfilment of the Great Commission and this aspect of Jesus' prophecy is within reach. World-wide persecution was only ever the case in the first two centuries (and then only in terms of the world as defined by the Roman Empire), before the conversion to Christianity of the Emperor Constantine in AD 312. Since then, it has never been the case in the Western world. But the rise of Islam in the Middle East, and its resurgence since oil became vital to the world, gave rise to persecution in territories (including some African nations) ruled by fundamentalist Islamic regimes. The dominance of Communism in the USSR and beyond led to fearful persecution for much of the twentieth century. This continues in China to this day. In other countries such as Burma, religious and political freedom are curtailed. It has been estimated that more Christians suffered for their faith in the twentieth century than in all the other centuries added together. (We must not forget that, sadly, Christians inflicted persecution on each other in the Catholic/Protestant struggles following the Reformation, perpetuated centuries later by extremists in Northern Ireland. There was also shameful persecution of Jews and Moslems by Christians, although some steps have been taken to repent of such blots on church history.) It could not be said that this aspect of Jesus' prophecy has been fulfilled as yet, although it is not in the least difficult to imagine a situation of persecution in the West in the near future. This could well be in the shape of laws enacted to curtail freedom to express the belief that Jesus is the only Lord. This could lead to apostasy by many, some of whom could be deceived by 'false prophets'. Compromise of the faith might well take the form of succumbing to the religious 'pick'n'mix' spirit of the age, instead of bowing the knee to the Spirit of the ages. These world-wide signs represent the intertwining of suffering and salvation, trial and triumph, grit and glory, vilification and vindication. Christians, filled with Christ's risen power, are called upon to take up the cross, until he comes in glory. But will it be a literal event?

A 'spiritual coming'?

Sadly, many theologians are agnostic about the Second Coming: they spiritualise the event itself, preferring to concentrate on the coming of the kingdom (and therefore the King) in the here and now. This is for various reasons: either they find the literal view so incredible that they believe there must be another interpretation, or, after careful research into what are known as the apocalyptic passages of Scripture (which we shall consider in the next paragraph), they regard the prophecies as referring to generalised trends in human history rather than dramatic supernatural intervention. Others focus on the problem raised by certain words of Jesus himself, in the context of having told his disciples about his return: 'I tell you the truth, this generation will certainly not pass away until all these things have happened' (Mark 13:30). As a result, some interpret his promise to return as having been fulfilled when the Holy Spirit came in power on the Day of Pentecost. They say that the apostles failed to realise that this was the explanation and mistakenly continued to prophesy the Second Coming after Pentecost, or else they believe that the whole of the age of the Church world-wide is the fulfilment of the Second Coming prophecies, and say that in Mark 13:30 Jesus was referring to the beginning of that age.

Is there a solution to these problems? If we take the last one first, there is no question that Mark 13:30 is a difficult verse to interpret, but various other meanings are possible. The most likely explanation is that, at this point in a long discourse, Jesus was directly answering the original question of the disciples which had given rise to it. As they were gazing at the remarkable architecture of the Jerusalem temple, Jesus commented that it would soon be destroyed. Some of the disciples asked him when this would happen. Jesus proceeded to prophesy not only about signs to look for in that connection, but beyond that, to even more cataclysmic events, culminating in his return. He then answered their question about the destruction of the temple (which took place forty years later, in AD 70). Jesus was in part trying to warn his hearers that one of the most devastating events in Jewish history would take place within a generation (which in Jewish reckoning was forty years).

The problem of apocalyptic language is more difficult to resolve. Apocalyptic writings began to emerge in Jewish literature after the time of the Old Testament prophets. These writers filled the vacuum left when no new prophets appeared on the scene, by writing works about alleged revelations from God, given through dreams, visions and heavenly journeys. These 'revelations' were just a literary device to convey a message to the author's contemporaries, using the pseudonym of an established prophet. The writers sometimes went to bizarre extremes in the use of symbolism. But their motive in interpreting history under the guise of prophecy was to reassure their contemporaries in times of great difficulty, that God was about to inaugurate his kingdom. Some scholars include the book of Daniel in this category. The problem is that Jesus, St Paul, St Peter and other New Testament writers used similar language at times, which makes it seem logical to interpret their 'prophecies' just as ways of writing about God working through the whole sweep of human history, and in particular contemporary circumstances of persecution, etc. We would want to assert that, while there can be no question of the influence and use of 'apocalyptic' language, this was powerfully transformed by the Holy Spirit in the New Testament, particularly in the book of Revelation, to be a vehicle conveying genuine prophecy about the future, which is not only generalised, but in some cases specific. This includes descriptions of the Second Coming, which will happen as a real event in history, bringing that history to an end and, no doubt, transcending all expectations. But how long do we have to wait?

The timing of the Second Coming

The followers, numbering about 50,000, of William Miller, an American farmer, firmly believed the world would end on 22 October 1844 – until it didn't. Perhaps not so many in the early 1990s still believed a seventeenth-century archbishop of Armagh, who predicted the same month and day, but in 1996! Both had made calculations from words and numbers in the Bible. A Polish nun, Sister Marie Gabriel, placed an advert in *The Times*, warning the world that planet Earth would be adversely affected by the comet which was to strike Jupiter in July 1994. It wasn't. Much to the relief of many, in 1995 the leaders of Jehovah's Witnesses put out a statement to the effect that, having got it wrong so often, they would no longer try to date the end of the world. A more recent scientific prediction was that the so-called 'Doomsday Asteroid' could strike the earth at 6.30 p.m. on 26 October 2028. There will be continuing calculation and speculation about that, until the actual date. In fact, any attempt to put a date to the Second Coming, or the end of the world, is doomed to failure. But this should not deter Christians from promoting expectation of the Second Coming. In the second epistle of Peter we read: 'you must understand that in the last days scoffers . . . will say, "Where is this 'coming' he promised? Ever since our fathers died, everything goes on as it has since the beginning of creation" ' (2 Pet. 3:3–4). If only we would take more notice of both the dramatic prophecies and the words of caution by Jesus himself. Having spoken about the signs mentioned above, and the shorter period of intense distress which would follow them, he said this:

> At that time the sign of the Son of Man will appear in the sky, and all the nations of the earth will mourn. They will see the

Son of Man coming on the clouds of the sky, with power and great glory . . . Now learn this lesson from the fig tree: as soon as its twigs get tender and its leaves come out, you know that summer is near. Even so, when you see all these things, you know that it is near, right at the door . . . Heaven and earth will pass away, but my words will never pass away. No one knows about that day or hour, not even the angels in heaven, nor the Son, but only the Father. (Matt. 24:30–6)

No further comment is necessary.

Chapter 5

Will there be another millennium?

'They will be priests of God and of Christ and will reign with him for a thousand years.'

(Rev. 20:6)

The new millennium

In January 1998, *The Times* newspaper published various letters about whether the millennial celebrations should be held at the beginning of the year 2001, rather than 2000. In one letter, M. L.West of All Souls College, Oxford, commented: 'It is not an anniversary that we shall be celebrating, because nothing whatever happened at either the beginning or the end of 1 BC (certainly not the birth of Jesus). What we are getting excited about is that *all the numbers will change*. It is like seeing 99,999 turn into 100,000 on the car mileometer. That's what it's all about.'!

There is a lot of truth in that, particularly as we know that the date of Jesus' birth was miscalculated in the sixth century by a monk (Dionysius Exiguus) who was ignorant of the dates of the reigns of the various Herods of biblical times. The two thousandth anniversary was probably in 1996. Irrespective of that, there is no particular reason why the passage from one thousand-year period to another should be specially significant. But the human race feels that it is, and uses it as an opportunity to look back and look ahead. Singling out one phenomenon only which gives people cause for concern, the twentieth century saw a population explosion, from just over two billion people to just under six billion. One projection into the new millennium is that there will be ten billion people alive in the year 2020, after which there could be a welcome reduction in the rate of growth. But the curve will still be upward, leaving one wondering just how many lives this planet can sustain. If distribution of resources were equitable, and exploitation and sheer greed kept in check, the probable answer is many more, but the reality is likely to be that millions more will be born into serious deprivation. If there is no solution to such massive problems, it is unlikely that the vast majority of humanity would be looking forward in the least to a new dawn one thousand years from now. But we trust that Jesus will have returned well before that time.

Maranatha

The shortest prayer in the Bible is 'Come, O Lord!' (1 Cor. 16:22). It is written in Aramaic, rather than the usual Greek – an indication of its early origin. The Aramaic is *Marana tha*. Christians in the West are usually reluctant to pray those words with much enthusiasm. Most live a relatively comfortable lifestyle, which they want their children to inherit. They don't want Jesus to come back, causing major disruption! Many are unaware that, by contrast, millions of believers are to be found in the two-thirds world who long for Jesus to return, to put to right the injustices of life which cause them so much suffering.

At the end of the book of Revelation, Jesus promises: 'Yes, I am coming soon', and the apostle John replies: 'Amen. Come, Lord Jesus' (Rev. 22:20). St Peter writes about looking forward to the day of God and speeding its coming (2 Pet. 3:12). It is a possibility that the date of Jesus' return is not set at all, but can be hastened or delayed, including by the Church. God does not want to send the divine Bridegroom for a reluctant Bride! He even delays, waiting for more people to repent (2 Pet. 3:9). On the other hand, the longer the delay, the greater the number of people who are born, requiring yet further evangelistic initiatives. Yet apathy, in addition to ignorance and confusion about the End

Times, do not serve to swell the ranks of Christians pleading with Jesus to come back. It would obviously be gross if we were to pray those words without at the same time working for the extension of God's kingdom here and now, whether by evangelism, loving care or campaigning against injustice. The Lord will turn a deaf ear to any plea for Jesus to return to right wrongs if we are not putting ourselves out to do the same in the present, even though aware that our efforts will only partially succeed. But we are being uncaring to the millions subjected to oppression of one form or another if we do not pray that prayer with fervency.

To be controversial, more could be achieved for the Lord's purposes if the Maranatha prayer were prayed regularly on a world-wide scale, than by thousands praying for revival. It is biblical to long and pray for Jesus to return. In the mysterious purposes of God, this could set in motion a chain of events (which might include revival), which will lead to the Second Coming. The consequences of such prayer are in the hands of God – we do not need to work out the complexities as to whether that means we are hastening persecution and judgment, as well as world-wide evangelisation and the glory of the actual event of Jesus' return. We would do well to look beyond, to the wonders of the new heavens and earth which would be the ultimate outcome. It is even possible that the return of God the Son is being delayed until God the Father sees such international intercession, inspired by God the Spirit.

The biblical Millennium

The story so far has been relatively uncomplicated. Admittedly, we have pointed out various different views about such matters as the whereabouts of heaven, or what is meant by hell. There is some uncertainty about the 'in-between' state (after death and before the Second Coming), except that those who have died will be with Christ. But the broad outline has seemed clear, as we have looked at Scripture, including that the resurrection of the body takes place when Jesus returns, after which there is the Last Judgment, prior to the creation of the new heaven and earth.

Now we turn to a major complicating factor! In the book of
Revelation, the writer appears to predict a special Millennium
when Christ will reign on earth, before the Last Judgment. This
is the most controversial aspect of eschatology. In fact, some
Christians have even separated from one another according to
their views on this subject. We shall try to show that such division
is unnecessary, even sinful, after attempting to describe the
different views in relatively simple terminology. It is important,
first of all, to look at the relevant biblical teaching. The only
clear description is in the book of Revelation:

> And I saw an angel coming down out of heaven . . . He seized
> the dragon, that ancient serpent, who is the devil, or Satan,
> and bound him for a thousand years. He threw him into the
> Abyss, and locked and sealed it over him, to keep him from
> deceiving the nations any more until the thousand years were
> ended. After that, he must be set free for a short time. I saw
> thrones on which were seated those who had been given
> authority to judge. And I saw the souls of those who had
> been beheaded because of their testimony for Jesus and
> because of the word of God. They had not worshipped the
> beast or his image and had not received his mark on their
> foreheads or their hands. They came to life and reigned with
> Christ for a thousand years. (The rest of the dead did not
> come to life until the thousand years were ended.) This is
> the first resurrection. Blessed and holy are those who have
> part in the first resurrection. The second death has no power
> over them, but they will be priests of God and of Christ and
> will reign with him for a thousand years. When the thousand
> years are over, Satan will be released from his prison and
> will go out to deceive the nations . . . They marched across
> the breadth of the earth and surrounded the camp of God's
> people, the city he loves. But fire came down from heaven
> and devoured them. And the devil, who deceived them, was
> thrown into the lake of burning sulphur, where the beast
> and the false prophet had been thrown. They will be
> tormented day and night for ever and ever. Then I saw a
> great white throne and him who was seated on it. Earth and

sky fled from his presence, and there was no place for them. (Rev. 20:1–11)

To summarise the main points made in this passage:

1 Satan is bound so that he is unable to deceive the nations.
2 Christian martyrs are raised, to reign with Christ for a thousand years.
3 Satan is released to deceive the nations once more.
4 The nations of the world pose a serious threat to the people of God.
5 They are overcome by supernatural intervention.
6 Satan is finally overthrown.
7 The Last Judgment follows.

This passage is followed by statements about the new heaven and earth, and preceded by what appears to be a description of the Second Coming. Jesus is pictured as a rider on a white horse, coming from heaven, followed by the armies of heaven, bringing judgment to the nations and ruling them with an 'iron sceptre' (Rev. 19:11–16).

Different views about the Millennium

First of all, we shall briefly describe the main views on this subject, looking first at the most literal interpretation of this passage. It is important to note that there is no similar teaching to be found elsewhere in the New Testament, although some would regard it as throwing light on a number of Old Testament passages. After that, we shall look at a possible synthesis.

The classic pre-millennial view
This seems to have been the view of the early Church, and there has been something of a renewal of interest in it recently in certain UK Christian circles. (We ourselves held conferences advocating this view, but more recently have been concerned to promote emphasis on all the subjects covered in this book, endeavouring to achieve mutual respect between those holding different views

on the Millennium.) It stresses the return of Jesus *before* ('*pre-*') he establishes his rule of a thousand years on earth. Those who hold this view would see the following order of events:

- Signs of the times take place.
- They lead to the manifestation of Antichrist and the seven-year Great Tribulation. (See the chapter on Revelation.)
- Christ returns both for and with the saints (some would say halfway through the seven-year tribulation), who are clothed in resurrection bodies. This is the 'first resurrection', including those who have been martyred for Christ, who will reign with Christ in the millennium.
- The Antichrist is destroyed.
- Satan is bound for a thousand years, making possible the Millennium: a thousand-year golden age of peace and righteousness, with evil being held in check, while Jesus reigns from Jerusalem. Believing Jews are prominent in his purposes.
- At the end of the Millennium Satan is released and there follows a final rebellion of evil which is crushed by the Lord.
- The devil is thrown into the lake of fire.
- The unbelieving dead are raised and the Last Judgment takes place, leading to hell for those without Christ.
- The new heaven and earth are created for God to dwell with those 'in Christ'.

Among the early Christian leaders (known as 'Fathers') who taught this view, applying it in different ways to contemporary events, were Irenaeus and Hippolytus. (Incidentally, all the Fathers whose views we know about expected the Church to go through the Great Tribulation. Yet some pre-millennialists today believe it will escape. They hold to the secret rapture theory, whereby the Church is removed before the tribulation.) For many centuries this view was replaced by another, but a German theologian, Johann Alsted, published a book, *The Beloved City*, in 1627, reviving the pre-millennial view. Edward Irving also taught a pre-millennial view in the nineteenth century, in reaction to the optimism of the many missionary societies, whose hope it was that the whole world would be christianised by God's grace through their efforts.

The post-millennial view

Those who hold this view believe that the passage in Revelation 19 about the rider on the white horse does not refer to the Second Coming, but to the power of Jesus displayed through his Church. They can therefore place this special Millennium before the Second Coming. Jesus therefore returns *after* ('*post*') the Millennium. When the Emperor Constantine converted to Christianity, leading to the christianisation of the Empire, many thought the Millennium had come. Some Christian teachers today believe that is still a valid interpretation: namely that, until the secularisation of the West, for well over a thousand years governments of the West (and initially of the Middle East too) overtly attempted to apply their understanding of Christian principles to society (even though with glaring imperfections). After that, Satan has been deceiving the nations, as prophesied in Revelation.

Daniel Whitby, Rector of St Edmund's, Salisbury, from 1669, taught that the Church would totally evangelise and then rule the world. This view was popularised through Jamieson, Fausset and Brown's *Commentary on the Bible*. The powerful world-wide missionary movement which gained ground in the nineteenth century was optimistic about a world-wide Christendom. This has been perpetuated in some circles, including missionary movements based in the States. Their modern optimistic version of the post-millennial view is that the world will be christianised in the (possibly near) future, leading to a Millennium – a long period of righteousness and peace – when evil will be reduced to a minimum and the majority of humanity will be converted. Then Christ will return and there will be resurrection, judgment, heaven and hell. This optimism is based on noting remarkable improvements in the last two thousand years: Christian principles have been widely accepted by many nations, even if they are not always put into practice. Slavery has largely disappeared. The status of women and children has greatly improved, as have social and economic conditions in many nations. There is much greater co-operation between the nations, and foreign aid is much in evidence. The Bible is widespread, while mass communications spread the gospel. Christianity has grown more in the last one hundred years than in the previous 1,800 – 28% of people in the world today are Christians. It is thought that false religions and philosophies will eventually fall before an aroused Christianity. (However, such views are often a eulogy of American achievements, and while not denying social improvements in some areas, this analysis of the world situation, and the hope of the golden age based upon it, seems unbalanced and unrealistic, ignoring the massive economic divide between first and third world, for example.)

Many (but not all) of those Christians who are currently praying for a world-wide revival hold to a form of post-millennialism. They are not naive about the state of the world as it is today, but believe that a world-wide outpouring of the Spirit would bring dramatic changes, ushering in an era when Jesus is acknowledged to be Lord of the nations. Some teach 'Reconstructionism', whereby the Old Testament principles for ordering Jewish life are re-applied to the whole world in the Millennium. Others teach 'Dominion' theology, believing the Holy Spirit is urging Christians to banish dark principalities and powers, so that the lordship of Christ might be displayed through the Church, including through political power being in the hands of Christians.

The a-millennial view

As we have seen, the pre-millennialism of the early Fathers was superseded initially by post-millennialism. Although there has been a revival of those two views, another view meanwhile came on the scene, as a reaction against the triumphalism which was based on the dominance of the Church in the post-Constantine era. This was a-millennialism, propounded by Augustine, which later became the view of many Protestant Reformers.

The NIV Study Bible (footnote on Rev. 20:2) describes the Millennium in this view as 'the present reign of the souls of deceased believers with Christ in heaven'. After his return, Christ will continue to 'reign over the perfect kingdom on the new earth in the eternal state', i.e. in heaven on earth. This interpretation teaches that there will be no period of universal peace and righteousness before the end. Good and evil will co-exist until the return of Christ. Revelation chapter 20 only refers to the present rule in heaven of believers who have died.

In this view, the defeat of Satan was in the first coming of Christ. The binding of Satan began then too. His influence is curtailed, not removed. There will be 'signs of the times' before the return of Christ, but those signs are to some degree already present. Immediately before the return of Christ these signs will be intensified. At Christ's return (which will be a single event) there will be a general resurrection of both believers and unbelievers. Believers who are still alive will be transformed, as will believers who have died. Then the final judgment will take place, followed by the new heavens and new earth. It is to these new heavens and new earth that the supposed Old Testament prophecies of the Millennium refer.

The dispensational view

A dispensationalist form of pre-millennialism was taught by John Nelson Darby, who left the Anglican ministry in 1827 to join the Brethren, a new Christian group at the time. It is important to know a little about this theory, because the complexities of dispensationalism produced an adverse reaction on the part of many young adults from a Brethren background in the 1970s, leading to some forming 'Housechurches' (later known as 'New Churches') in the UK. Preferring to stress the extension of God's kingdom in the present, their enthusiasm led to a movement which had attracted 250,000 adherents (mainly from existing denominations) by the end of the twentieth century, changing the face of the British church scene. Although many of the leaders now believe in the classic pre-millennial view (while some moved on in their thinking to one of the other views), there was at first an understandable reaction against eschatology, which meant that there was little emphasis for many years in most of those circles on the return of Jesus and related subjects. But the dispensational view continues to be prevalent in many Pentecostal churches and in fundamentalist church circles in the States.

Darby greatly influenced Cyrus Ingerson Scofield who was ordained into the American Congregational ministry in 1882. The latter produced the Scofield Reference Bible, which has sold over two million copies since it was published in 1909. It is this Bible which popularised dispensational pre-millennialism. Since it has influenced so many Christians, we provide an outline of this view, although there are many variations which make it even more complex.

There are seven dispensations (different ways in which God deals with humanity). In each of these eras God made a distinct covenant, 'dispensing' his relationship with humanity on that basis. The seven dispensations are:

1 *The dispensation of innocence* – Creation to the Fall (Edenic).
2 *The dispensation of conscience* – the Fall to the Flood (Antediluvian).
3 *The dispensation of human government* – the Flood to Babel (Noahic).
4 *The dispensation of promise* – the call of Abraham to giving of the Law (Abrahamic).
5 *The dispensation of law* – giving of the Law until the death of Christ, tearing of temple veil and Jewish rejection of Messiah (Mosaic).
6 *The dispensation of grace* – the Cross to the rapture of the Church (Apostolic). The rapture is sudden, unexpected and secret. It takes place when Christ returns to meet the saints in the air. This first return of Christ is known only to believers. The raptured Church will face the judgment seat of Christ but it will miss the tribulation. (Some dispensationalists have taught a partial rapture, with only believers who are spiritually prepared for it being included. Also, some have taught a mid-tribulational rapture, normally halfway through the seven-year tribulation.)
7 *The dispensation of the kingdom or the millennium* – the Second Coming to the final satanic revolt (Millennial).

This last stage includes the following details:

- After the rapture Christ will return once more, on this occasion publicly, to the Mount of Olives with his saints. (In this view, there are two future comings of Christ: one secret and unexpected, one public, heralded by signs.)
- Christ will win the battle of Armageddon and overthrow the trinity of evil: Satan, the antichrist and the beast. Satan will be bound for a thousand years.
- Righteousness will fill the earth.
- The Holy Spirit will cause the Jews to accept Christ's death for their national salvation
- The Gentiles who treated Israel well during the tribulation will join Israel in the Millennium, but will be subservient to Israel.
- Israel will head the nations in worship (centred on a glorious new temple) in this golden age of peace and righteousness. So the promises in the Old Testament to Israel will be literally fulfilled.
- The Church will remain in heaven during the Millennium.
- At the end of the Millennium Satan will be released and deceive many.
- This rebellion will be crushed by the Lord and will lead to the great white throne judgment, resulting in Satan, his angels and unbelievers being destroyed.
- God will create the new heavens and new earth.

Distinctive features of the tribulation
During this seven-year period of great tribulation (the seventieth 'week' of Daniel 9:24–7):

- the seals, trumpets and bowls judgments of Revelation will take place;
- the remnant of the Jews, brought back to their land in unbelief, will be saved;
- the nominal church remaining on earth during the tribulation will fall into apostasy;
- eventually the nations will gather against Israel.

Division between the Church and Israel
A key point in dispensationalism is that believing Israel takes over from the Church during the Millennium, after Christians have been raptured to be with Christ.

Different gospel messages
1 The gospel of the kingdom: the news about an earthly kingdom of Israel (initially preached by Jesus until the Jews rejected him). In this view, many of the parables were only relevant at this stage.
2 The gospel of the grace of God: that Jesus died and rose again (preached by Jesus after the Jews rejected him and by the apostles).
3 Paul's gospel: an expansion of the gospel of grace including revelation of the 'mystery' of the Church.
4 The everlasting gospel: this is preached by the Jews in the tribulation, after the rapture. It is news that all who are saved in the tribulation will enter the millennial Kingdom.

Mutual respect

After looking at all these different views, it is little wonder that most Christian teachers decide to avoid the subject of the Millennium. Unfortunately, this has led to teaching about the return of Christ being neglected too, even though it is mentioned over three hundred times in the New Testament and is referred to in the historic creeds of the Church. However, two approaches ought to be possible. One is to encourage those who strongly hold a particular view at least to recognise that most of those with a different view are endeavouring to be true to Scripture, and therefore are to be respected, even though disagreement may obviously still be expressed. The other is to attempt a synthesis, based on aspects of the major views. At a consultation on the subject convened by us, there were theologians and Christian leaders representing the first three views, who, after listening to one another, were able to respect the integrity of all present. More than that, there was recognition of the helpful differences of emphasis of the major millennial positions, and even a constructive attempt to achieve a synthesis over key issues relating to the End Times. We shall include those points in the last chapter, but here will attempt to show pros and cons of each view, before hinting at a way of holding the 'pre', 'post' and 'a' positions together!

Strengths and weaknesses

The classic pre-millennial view is strong on taking the biblical teaching on the subject at face value, without making as much of every detail as the dispensationalists. It is realistic in stressing that the only possibility of international recognition of the lordship of Christ could be after his return in glory, while realising that there can only be perfection when all evil, and death itself, has finally been banished prior to the new creation. However, it leaves many unsolved problems, such as how there can be death and imperfections during the time of the millennial reign of Jesus. There is also danger of the pitfall (although many who hold this view do *not* fall into it), of being soft on extending God's kingdom here and now, while waiting for the return of Jesus and the millennium.

It is a strength of *the dispensational view* that it attempts to make sense of every single reference to the relevant subjects in Scripture, including the Old Testament passages, which are important. Belief in a secret rapture certainly encourages expectation of the imminent return of Christ. It also emphasises helpful teaching on the various covenants in Scripture, and other important matters. However, it takes too literally every detail, which is not necessary; in taking these to a logical conclusion, it teaches several versions of the gospel message, which is unhelpful to say the least; teaching about a rapture of believers is resonant of escapism, which is not the way of the cross; the place of the Jewish people in God's purposes seems to be divorced from the Church and even given pre-eminence; and the rigid description and timetable of events leaves no room for the possibility that the reality of the Second Coming, as the first, will transcend all expectations.

The post-millennial view has different strengths, according to the variations of it. Those who regard the first several centuries AD (some would take the thousand years literally, others would be more flexible) as being the Millennium, certainly take seriously the massive impact which the gospel made on the Roman Empire, changing for ever the course of European history, with consequences which eventually impacted the whole world. Those who believe that an even better Christendom is still to come this side of the Second Coming must have amazing optimism, particularly after two world wars centred on Europe. However, Christians with such views obviously have deep motivation to influence social and political change for Christ. Those who link that with world-wide evangelisation or even revival are usually at the forefront of intercessory movements for revival, or campaigns for evangelism on an international scale. But it would be misleading to give the impression that they leave their pre-millennial sisters and brothers behind on those two issues, because belief in the imminence of the return of Jesus also provides strong incentive for evangelism, whereas post-millennialists sense no such urgency, except the knowledge that each individual has to stand before God one day. In fact, they do not expect Jesus to return until Christianity has ruled OK! They believe Christ will exercise his reign through the Church. This unfortunately can lead some to exaggerate claims about the power of believers to deal with the forces of darkness. It is dangerous for Christians to try to banish evil powers over areas of life where there is no willingness, on the part of those on the receiving end of such prayers, to welcome Jesus as Lord. Many Christians have become disillusioned about God's authority exercised through them, because of such misunderstandings. Although there are amazing promises in the Bible about the power of the Holy Spirit available to the children of God, these need to be held in tension with scriptures about carrying the cross.

The a-millennial view, by contrast, embodies an important understanding of the paradox that, on the one hand, Jesus has already overcome evil, and this victory may well be displayed through some individual believers, some local churches, or even in some areas of life or some geographical regions where his lordship is acknowledged. But, on the other hand, evil flourishes, and the sovereignty of Christ will not be fully realised until the next life. Meanwhile those who have died 'in Christ' reign with him in heaven. Whereas there is much truth in this, it does not seem to take seriously the emphasis in Revelation 20, that Satan is prevented from deceiving *the nations* for a thousand years. But many of those who hold this view usually spiritualise passages about the Great Tribulation too, thus having the advantage of believing that Jesus could return at any time, without the need for certain events to take place in history first.

A possible solution

There is no reason at all why an attempt should not be made to take the best of all views! This might be described as *pan-millennialism*, although that description has been current for some time as a joke, that it will all pan out in the end! This view of ours attempts to apply the principles of interpreting prophecy in Scripture to Revelation 20, namely: multiple reference, the concertina effect, dual aspect and purposive characteristics.

We would want to take seriously the historical post-millennial view, that there was an initial, partial fulfilment through the establishment of Christendom. There is also obviously truth in the a-millennial concept of the reign of Christ throughout history, and a possibility that believers who have died are presently exercising delegated reign with him in heaven now. *No one can rule out* the possibility of future world-wide revival, ushering in a new 'Christendom' (the future post-millennial view), particularly after reading about past or present revivals which have transformed regions or even nations. Revival (a time when God works in a special way, resulting in large numbers of people turning to the faith) usually occurs unexpectedly, in surprising places or situations. Historians believe that the nation-wide revival of Christianity, largely through the influence of John Wesley, in eighteenth-century Britain, prevented the equivalent of the French Revolution here. The after-effects included subsequent revivals both here and in the USA and beyond, leading to the world-wide missionary movement. A revival which is profoundly affecting the nation has been taking place in

Argentina since the Falklands war. But some think that similar revivals are *unlikely* in the post-Christian West. If so, one view, which we think has potential, is to think of 'Christendom' (the rule of Christ deeply affecting national life) as being exemplified in different nations at different times in history.

Our opinion of whether there will be revival in the Western Church is that the situation is vastly different in post-Christian nations from the rest of the world. We think that a spiritual awakening is already taking place in the West, after the sterility of the 1960s–1980s, but it is a New Age mixture. Rather than being fearful of this phenomenon, Christians should use every opportunity which is presented by greater openness to witness to their faith in culturally sensitive ways, while warning against syncretism with the occult or pantheism. However, we think it unlikely that a new Christendom will be established once again in what are post-Christian nations, by contrast with what could happen in nations which have never previously embraced the gospel on a wide scale. Certainly there could be revival elsewhere in the world, at the very least (and it is already happening in some places). The prophecy of Jesus about world-wide evangelism was that the 'gospel of the kingdom [would] be preached in the whole world as a *testimony* to all nations, and then the end [would] come' (Matt. 24:14). He did not say that every nation would be converted to Christianity towards 'the end', but that all would be given the opportunity. The implication is that many individuals would respond (and possibly *some* nations, in the sense of their government and national laws and life being deeply influenced by Christian principles). Certainly in the book of Revelation we read that some 'from every tribe and language and people and nation' have been 'purchased' for God by the death of Jesus (Rev. 5:9).

Since the prophecies of Jesus and in Revelation stress judgments, it is likely that there will be a mixture of revival and judgment, blessing and persecution, as the End Times draw to a close. This could lead to a brief time of intense tribulation, prior to the return of Christ. The place of the Jewish people in all this will be discussed in a later chapter. We have therefore demonstrated that it is possible to hold together aspects of post-

and a-millennial views, including the possibility of future revival(s), before a final conflict between good and evil. But where does pre-millennialism fit into the picture: namely, that the return of Jesus ushers in an earthly Millennium, in addition to the initial fulfilments of the Revelation 20 prophecy? This brings in the matter of the *purpose* of the prophecy about the Millennium.

A suggested reason for an earthly reign of Christ

The focus in Revelation 20 appears to be connected with *the nations of the world*. In chapter 19 we read that (according to the pre-millennial view) the approach of the return of Christ sparks off the ultimate conflict between good and evil, God and the devil, the people of God and the agents of Satan, including all human powers and authorities which are opposed to the will of God. This comes to a head in the battle of Armageddon, described in that chapter, but only mentioned by name in Rev. 16:14–16: 'spirits of demons . . . go out to the kings of the whole world, to gather them for the battle on the great day of God Almighty. "Behold, I come like a thief!" . . . Then they gathered the kings together to the place that in Hebrew is called Armageddon.' This mass rebellion of the nations against God is followed by the binding of Satan's power 'to keep him from deceiving the nations any more until the thousand years were ended' (Rev. 20:3). That demonstration of God's power over the devil makes it possible for Christ to rule with the resurrected martyred saints. The implication is that this rule is over the nations, because we read that 'When the thousand years are over, Satan will be released from his prison and will go out to deceive the nations in the four corners of the earth' (Rev. 20:7). *It is our view that whatever previous partial fulfilments there may have been of the prophecy about a millennial reign of Jesus on earth (whether in early Christendom, or throughout history, or at different periods in different nations, or still to come but prior to the Second Coming), there will be one ultimate fulfilment when Jesus returns to planet Earth. Its purpose will be to demonstrate Christ's sovereignty over the nations, i.e. the way in which human society is ordered in a corporate sense.* This human authority, which has such influence for good or ill over the life of every person who has ever lived, is regarded in the Bible as delegated from God (Rom. 13:1), and therefore ought to have been exercised in accordance with his purposes for humanity. Jurgen Moltmann, a theologian who has made a major contribution to the modern study of eschatology in academic circles, is convinced of the importance of a millennial reign of Christ. Just one quotation from p. 201 of *The Coming of God* (SCM, 1996) must suffice: 'Without millenarian hope, the Christian ethic of resistance and the consistent discipleship of Christ lose their most powerful motivation. Without the expectation of an alternative kingdom of Christ, the community of Christ loses its character as "contrast community" to society.'

The lordship of Christ has already been, and will continue to be, amply demonstrated in the lives of *individuals*, who welcome his Holy Spirit into their lives (and over every individual at the Last Judgment). It is partially demonstrated now in *the Church*, and will be perfectly when the Bridegroom (Jesus) returns for his Bride. It will also be demonstrated over the whole of earthly *creation*, when the new earth is created. But the millennial reign of Christ is about his lordship over *the nations*. If that were not to be perfectly demonstrated, then evil would have triumphed in the present order, which seems to undermine the completeness of the victory won at the cross. In fact the world as corporately organised would never otherwise acknowledge or submit to God. (In another chapter we look at the question of whether Jesus also demonstrates his authority in a particular way, over Israel.) Scripture also hints at the ultimate manifestation of God's sovereignty through his Son over the entire *universe*, which may be at the time of the creation of a new earth, or may be millions of years hence.

All this is described in Colossians 1:15–20:

He [the Son] is the image of the invisible God, the firstborn over all creation. For by him all things were created: things in heaven and on earth, visible and invisible, whether thrones or powers or rulers or authorities; all things were created by him and for him. He is before all things, and in him all things hold together. And he is the head of the body, the church; he is the beginning and the firstborn from among the dead, so that in everything he might have the supremacy. For God was pleased to have all his fulness dwell in him, and through him to reconcile to himself all things, whether things on earth or things in heaven, by making peace through his blood, shed on the cross.

The demonstration of God's sovereignty over the nations may only be for a brief period, but it will certainly be an era in itself. We see no need to regard the thousand-year period as literal in length. The numbers in Revelation are symbolic, e.g. seven refers to completeness, twelve to the people of Israel (because of the original twelve tribes) or the Church (because of the original twelve apostles) and one thousand may refer to an epoch. In 2 Peter 3:8 we read, 'With the Lord a day is like a thousand years, and a thousand years are like a day.' After the Millennium, there is a last revolt, due to rebellion against God being so ingrained in the nations of the world, leading to his ultimate destruction of all evil (Rev. 20:7–10). Although at first sight it seems incredible that there could be an uprising in the earthly reign of Christ himself, it is in the purposes of God, to pave the way for the new heaven and earth. In these ways, the Lord of glory shows his sovereignty over all earthly lords and all supernatural lords, after which the Creator demonstrates his supremacy over the entire created order. There are therefore three stages of Christ's reign, in addition to his reign in heaven:

1 The partially hidden kingdom on earth between the two advents;
2 The relatively brief manifest kingdom on earth (the Millennium) after the second advent;
3 The glorious kingdom on the new earth after the Last Judgment.

Meanwhile, in the 'now', before the 'not yet', we pray: 'Your kingdom come, your will be done on earth as it is in heaven.'

Chapter 6

Does the Old Testament shed light on the future?

'For prophecy never had its origin in the will of man, but men spoke from God as they were carried along by the Holy Spirit.'

(2 Pet. 1:21)

Many Christians these days scarcely ever read the Old Testament. They regard it as irrelevant, difficult to understand and boring. It is a Jewish book, interesting (so the reasoning goes) only to those who want to understand more about Jewish history and literature, or who want to dig around the roots of Christianity to examine its origins. As for the prophetic books, they seem largely incomprehensible to many a person in the pew. It is a great pity that such people miss out on some of the most dramatic story-telling in literature, some of the most beautiful poetry, some of the deepest insights into the nature of the one true God, who keeps on loving, even though spurned time and again by his chosen people.

Not only does the Old Testament contain much to challenge us in the present, but it comes alive when understood as a collection of books which, through the inspiration of the Holy Spirit, contains a message about the future. When the risen Jesus walked along the road to Emmaus with two disciples he said:

'How foolish you are, and how slow of heart to believe all that the prophets have spoken! . . . And beginning with Moses and all the Prophets, he explained to them what was said in all the Scriptures concerning himself' (Luke 24:25, 27). What a Bible study that must have been! No doubt he showed from the first five books of the Bible (the books of Moses) that God had chosen to bring blessing to the world through the descendants of Abraham – who was, of course, the ancestor of Jesus. He would have revealed how the sacrificial ritual instituted by Moses, which underlined the seriousness of sin and the need for a remedy, in fact pointed forward prophetically to the cross; how in the historical books, the Psalms and the Prophets, there are many references to a greater king even than David, whose kingdom would be everlasting. All this is but a fraction of the prophetic nature of the Old Testament, much of which the reader can see (with the benefit of hindsight) has already been fulfilled in Jesus. There are also fascinating glimpses into events still future, as the significance of Jesus for the world continues to unfold. Some of these revelations are, as one would expect, in the books we call the prophetic books (Isaiah–Malachi, comprising the last third of the Old Testament), but they are also to be found in the historical and poetic books. It is hoped that a whirlwind tour of the Old Testament, highlighting its prophetic message, will also open up some other aspects of this literature, helping the reluctant reader to see that it is very important not only to the Jewish race, but to Christianity. Before we embark on that, more needs to be said about biblical prophecy.

Prophecy in the Bible

Soothsayers, fortune-tellers and the like are condemned in Scripture, because they attempt to discover or predict the future using human or occult powers, and do so for their own ends (or, if for the 'benefit' of others, not with the motive of bringing glory to God). Their predictions are usually unconditional, and if they contain a negative element can lead people into deep fear. By contrast, prophecy inspired by the Holy Spirit is only revealed with a divine purpose in mind (never just to satisfy curiosity about the future), and if it contains a predictive element, it is nearly always conditional on the response of the recipients – there is nothing fatalistic about it. There are occasions when God pronounces that the judgment predicted is irreversible, but only after he has already given many opportunities to repent, to no avail. The outcome is therefore always affected by the response of the people of God.

Biblical prophecy about the future may be about the big issues for humanity, such as those dealt with in this book, or about what might happen to a nation, or town, or even an individual. Many prophets would have had only a hazy notion about how their words would be fulfilled. The exact outcome was not their responsibility – they were expected only to utter their God-given message. But in so doing, as an act of faith, they contributed to the outworking of the purposes of God. This is a mystery, but so is intercessory prayer. Biblical prophecy is forthtelling as well as foretelling. In other words, God speaks into the contemporary situation, revealing something of his nature, his relationship with his people, his pleasure over their obedience, but displeasure when they turn from his will and his ways. Through his servants the prophets he proclaims his love and holiness, with consequent requirements for his people to reflect his nature, including his justice. In fact, many scholars try to limit prophecy to this important element, whereas it may clearly be seen from Genesis to Revelation that foretelling the future is also a strong element in biblical prophecy.

Woven throughout the Bible are prophecies connected with Christ, including those about his first and second comings. After all, the one who is the Alpha and Omega, the beginning and the end, the agent of creation, the one in whose person the entire universe will be reconciled, is bound to pervade the messages of the prophets. Biblical prophecy about Jesus should be seen not so much as attempts to see into the future, however inspired, but rather the result of the Holy Spirit fulfilling his role to point to the Lord of history, who dwells at one and the same time in the past, present and future. It is impossible for divinely inspired writings, taken as a whole, to do anything other than reveal Christ. His story began even before creation and will continue beyond the end of time. The awesome power of his person inevitably breaks through into the present, whenever that present might be.

Genesis

Pointers about the future are seen even in the creation narratives, but more details begin to emerge from Genesis chapter 12 onwards, when God chose one man, then one nation, to be the vehicle of his revelation. It is fascinating that nearly four thousand years ago, the one Creator God revealed himself to a man called Abram, born and bred surrounded by Mesopotamian culture and religion, giving him a prophetic revelation which is still being fulfilled to this day. This illustrates one of the ways in which prophecy is conveyed in the historical books: through a promise of God about the future. 'The LORD had said . . . "Leave your country, your people and your father's household and go to the land I will show you. I will make you into a great nation and I will bless you; I will make your name great, and you will be a blessing . . . and all peoples on earth will be blessed through you"' (Gen. 12:1–3). Abram, later to be renamed Abraham, was to become the founder member of the Jewish race, into which Jesus was eventually born, as a result of whose life, death and resurrection many millions of lives have been transformed. From the time when that ancient prophecy was given, the Jewish people before Christ lived to see a partial fulfilment of the promised blessing; we in the Church have seen more of it as the gospel has spread across the globe; but we look forward to its completion, sure in the knowledge that God is faithful in fulfilling his promises.

Another way in which prophecy is conveyed through history is when God brings about a series of events which foreshadow later developments. For instance, most Christians are familiar with the dramatic story in Genesis of how Abraham was on the point of sacrificing his only son, Isaac, in obedience to what he believed was God's command. Such an instruction would not have seemed strange to his ears (as child-sacrifice was not uncommon in the rituals of some of the religions of the day) were it not for the impossibility of God's promise to him being fulfilled if his only son and heir died. His faith was being tested to the limit. The dramatic story continues in Genesis 22:7–18:

> Isaac spoke up and said to his father Abraham, 'Father?' 'Yes, my son?' Abraham replied. 'The fire and wood are here,' Isaac said, 'but where is the lamb for the burnt offering?' Abraham answered, 'God himself will provide the lamb for the burnt offering, my son.' And the two of them went on together. When they reached the place God had told him about, Abraham built an altar there and arranged the wood on it. He bound his son Isaac and laid him on the altar, on top of the wood. Then he reached out his hand and took the knife to slay his son. But the angel of the LORD called out to him from heaven, 'Abraham! Abraham!' 'Here I am,' he replied. 'Do not lay a hand on the boy,' he said. 'Do not do anything to him. Now I know that you fear God, because you have not withheld from me your son, your only son.' Abraham looked up and there in a thicket he saw a ram caught by its horns. He went over and took the ram and sacrificed it as a burnt offering instead of his son. So Abraham called that place The LORD Will Provide . . . The angel of the LORD called to Abraham . . . a second time [there follows a repetition of the original prophecy].

This story is typical of many which are fascinating in themselves; are important to Jewish history; contain a message relevant to the reader; but also are seen by Christians as clearly foreshadowing God's purposes in Jesus, including his sacrificial death. It was only in Jesus that both the sacrifice of a son and the provision of a lamb were brought together, so making it possible for the nations of the earth to be blessed (through the salvation of millions of individuals and in other ways, such as the laws of many nations being influenced by Judaeo–Christian standards). It is important to say that it is neither necessary nor helpful to treat most events recorded in the Old Testament as prophetic allegories about Christ, as some have done. But some have such clear relevance that it would be obtuse to ignore the dual reference

– the prophetic significance, as well as the historical aspect. This is called typology, where events were real in history, but can subsequently be seen to foreshadow God's later actions, uniting past and future in his purposes.

Incidentally, lest some are shocked that God deliberately allowed Abraham to believe that he wanted him to sacrifice his child, it is worth noting not only that God knew he had planned the provision of the ram, but that it illustrates one of God's methods of teaching deep truths. That is, he starts with the present understanding or customs of the individual or group, then moves them on by a surprising or shocking new idea or incident. (An example of the latter was Jesus' ride into Jerusalem, which fitted the Messianic expectations of the day, only for that to be followed by the scandal of the cross, revealing a very different kind of Messiah, or Christ.)

Exodus

The same pattern, of promises which were soon partially fulfilled, foreshadowed later events, yet still await complete fulfilment, can be seen in the stories surrounding the Exodus. It was famine which forced the twelve great-grandchildren of Abraham to leave the Promised Land and settle in Egypt. One of them, Joseph, who after initial ill-treatment became Pharaoh's right-hand man, has been seen by some commentators as a foreshadowing of Christ, because he was used by God through suffering, then promotion, to rescue his people from almost certain demise. But little did he and his brothers realise that it would be several centuries before their descendants would return to the land which God had promised to their father, Jacob, in his famous dream, of

> a stairway resting on the earth, with its top reaching to heaven, and the angels of God were ascending and descending on it. There above it stood the LORD, and he said: '. . . All peoples on earth will be blessed through you and your offspring. I am with you and will watch over you wherever you go, and I will bring you back to this land. I will not leave you until I have done what I have promised you.' (Gen. 28:12–15)

Long after the Pharaoh who promoted Joseph had died, another Pharaoh came to power, who oppressed the Israelites, using them as slave labour. There follows one of the most dramatic periods in Israelite history: the story of the baby Moses found in the bulrushes by Pharaoh's daughter; Moses' escape to Midian after killing an Egyptian whom he saw beating up a Hebrew slave; the revelation by God to Moses at the burning bush that he is 'I am who I am'; his challenge to Moses to demand from Pharaoh: 'Let my people go'; the destructive plagues viewed as judgment on Pharaoh's intransigence; the final terror of the angel of death slaying all the firstborn. What happened next is remembered to this day in the Passover festival, to commemorate the time when the destroying angel *passed over* all the households of the Israelites who had killed a lamb, daubing its blood on their door frames. In 1 Corinthians 5:7–8, St Paul writes: 'For Christ, our Passover lamb, has been sacrificed. Therefore let us keep the Festival . . . with . . . sincerity and truth.' Some Gentile Christians, and nearly all Messianic (Jewish) believers, celebrate a christianised version of the Passover, which the New Testament makes abundantly clear found the true fulfilment of its significance in the death of Jesus. Those who by faith claim the protection of his blood (the benefits for the world of his death) are saved from spiritual death. But the reason most Christians celebrate holy communion rather than the original Passover is that Jesus reinterpreted both the ceremonial and its significance, when he took the cup and broke the bread in the middle of the Passover celebration, on the eve of his crucifixion.

In the wilderness

After the Passover, the great deliverance through the Red Sea took place, which has been likened to the greater salvation which was accomplished by Jesus. The sacrifices (described in the book of Leviticus and elsewhere) which were instituted in the wilderness wanderings are consistently interpreted in the New Testament as pointing forward to and being fulfilled in Jesus. The letter to Hebrews was written mainly to show Jewish believers how Christ was the fulfilment of the ritual law –

he was, in the wonderful purposes of God, both priest and sacrifice:

> When Christ came as high priest of the good things that are already here . . . He did not enter by means of the blood of goats and calves; but he entered the Most Holy Place once for all by his own blood, having obtained eternal redemption. The blood of goats and bulls and the ashes of a heifer sprinkled on those who are ceremonially unclean sanctify them so that they are outwardly clean. How much more, then, will the blood of Christ, who through the eternal Spirit offered himself unblemished to God, cleanse our consciences from acts that lead to death, so that we may serve the living God! (Heb. 9:11–14)

Various incidents in the wilderness (described in the books of Exodus, Numbers and Deuteronomy) are reinterpreted in the New Testament for the benefit of the first disciples, or early Church. It seems that historical events, or God-given ritual, or special covenants, were deliberately planned by God partly to have prophetic significance, pointing forward usually to Christ's life, death and resurrection, or other vital truths, but sometimes beyond that, even to the End Times. During the time in the wilderness, there was also an extraordinary incident when God used a pagan seer to utter a prophecy of blessing on the Israelites, so defying the wishes of his king, who had ordered him to put a curse on them. His messages include a prediction about a powerful ruler arising in Israel in the future. This is usually interpreted as referring initially to David, then to Christ:

> Come, let me warn you of . . . days to come [*'Latter Days'* – *literally 'at the end of the days'* – *the first appearance of this significant phrase in the Bible*] . . . 'The oracle of Balaam son of Beor, the oracle of one whose eye sees clearly, the oracle of one who hears the words of God, who has knowledge from the Most High, who sees a vision from the Almighty, who falls prostrate, and whose eyes are opened: I see him, but not now; I behold him, but not near. A star will come out of Jacob;

a sceptre will rise out of Israel . . . his enemy, will be conquered, but Israel will grow strong. A ruler will come out of Jacob and destroy the survivors of the city.' (Num. 24:14–19)

Covenants and laws

The Old Testament is about God's covenants, or binding agreements, with the nation of Israel to which he had chosen to reveal himself, with the intention that they would share that revelation with the rest of the world. There are a series of covenants, each one pointing forward to and being developed in the next. In that sense, they are prophetic. All of them lead up to an even greater covenant with redeemed humanity – the New Covenant, which is what the New Testament is all about. That is why it is impossible to understand the Old Testament without looking at it through prophetic spectacles. God never intended to continue to channel his revelations and his dealings with humanity through one nation. That would have been far too restrictive. It began that way, because the original rebellion of the first man and woman led, over successive generations, to such a mountain of sin piling up that God allowed the entire human race, except for Noah's family, to be destroyed by a flood. From that point on, God's plan was to choose one man, then one tribe, then one nation, then the Church (incorporating Jew and Gentile) to be the vehicles of knowledge about the one true God and his ways. The covenant with Noah was followed, as we have seen, by the covenant with Abraham. This was made more elaborate in a covenant with his descendants, the Israelites, revealed through Moses:

For you are a people holy to the LORD your God. The LORD your God has chosen you out of all the peoples on the face of the earth to be his people, his treasured possession . . . Know therefore that the LORD your God is God; he is the faithful God, keeping his covenant of love to a thousand generations of those who love him and keep his commands. (Deut. 7:6, 9)

This covenant was preceded by an astonishing prophecy of the exile of the Jews to Babylon, and their return, in Deuteronomy 4:25–32. This did not take place until the sixth century BC.

Judges and kings

Once the Israelites had settled in the Promised Land, as described in the book of Joshua, their history is one of continual renewal, rebellion, repentance and restoration. Through Moses, God had provided them not only with a system of sacrifices, including the Day of Atonement (described in Leviticus 16, when provision was made through sacrifice for the forgiveness of the sins of the people committed in the previous year), but with a series of laws to govern their national life. Rewards for obedience to God, and punishment for disobedience (including, in extreme circumstances, being banished from their land), are clearly spelt out. The Israelites eventually tired of a series of judges (some of whom were also prophets) being appointed to call them back to God's ways. They demanded that Samuel, the last of the prophet/ judges, should appoint a king like those of the surrounding nations. When the greatest king of all – David – came to the throne, the prophet Nathan predicted: 'Your house and your kingdom shall endure for ever before me; your throne shall be established for ever.' This 'Davidic Covenant' was fulfilled through David's descendant, Jesus, in a way which was unforeseen so many centuries before. After the reign of his son, Solomon, the nation of Israel descended into civil war, as a result of which it was divided into two. Good and bad kings followed as described in the books of Kings and Chronicles, some leading the people of God so far astray in ways of idolatry and immorality that God allowed first the northern kingdom of Israel to be defeated by the Assyrians in 722 BC, then the southern kingdom, Judah, including Jerusalem, to fall to the Babylonians in 586 BC. Unlike his people, God always keeps his positive promises, and also fulfils the prophecies, both positive and negative, which he gives through his servants. Only repentance averts judgment, as Israel and Judah discovered through bitter experience. While there is no space to give more examples of accurate predictions about the future of the Jewish people, enough has been said so far to show that the prophetic aspect of the historical books of the Old Testament should be taken very seriously.

Job and the Psalms

As we move from history to the poetic writings, we begin to glimpse the insights of the time into subjects such as life after death. Understanding was fairly embryonic, but occasionally there is a revelation which is much more fully developed. In the middle of Job's agonising about his many troubles, he suddenly exclaims: 'I know that my Redeemer lives, and that in the end he will stand upon the earth. And after my skin has been destroyed, yet in my flesh I will see God; I myself will see him with my own eyes – I, and not another. How my heart yearns within me!' (Job 19:25–7) The Psalmist exclaims: 'you will not abandon me to the grave, nor will you let your Holy One see decay' (Ps. 16:10). In fact, verses 8–11 were quoted by St Peter in his Pentecost sermon, as referring to Christ's resurrection (Acts 2:25–8), and he went on to quote Psalm 110 as predicting the ascension. By contrast, Psalm 22 is a vivid prophetic description (although we are not suggesting that the writer understood it as such) of the crucifixion, the first sentence of which Jesus quoted on the cross, when he cried out: 'My God, my God, why have you forsaken me?' Psalm 72 is interpreted as referring not only to the reign of Solomon, but to the future Messianic kingdom, e.g. 'He will . . . save the children of the needy; he will crush the oppressor. He will endure as long as the sun . . . through all generations' (72:4–5). These ideas reach even greater heights in Psalm 96, which ends with the majestic words: 'Then all the trees of the forest will sing for joy; they will sing before the LORD, for he comes, he comes to judge the earth. He will judge the world in righteousness and the peoples in his truth.'

The prophets

Our jet-flight over the Old Testament, where we have taken particular notice of the prophetic aspect, has now reached the books which major on prophecy. The big four (Isaiah, Jeremiah, Ezekiel and Daniel) are in some ways easier to follow than the twelve minor prophetic books. That is partly because the former happen to have been included in the correct chronological order, whereas that is not the case with the 'minor prophets'. The simplest way of finding one's bearings is to remember the two most traumatic dates in the history of the Jews before Christ – 722 and 586 BC. Those dates respectively are when Samaria, the capital of Israel, and Jerusalem, the capital of Judah, were conquered. The unthinkable happened: God removed his protection from his people – the only nation, or twin-nations, in the world to which the Creator God had revealed his will in any detail. He had progressively revealed more of his nature and his ways to them, so that they could testify to the surrounding nations about his love and power. Prophet after prophet was sent by God to encourage, challenge, warn and eventually pronounce judgment. This was because of the numerous sins of the people, which could be summarised in three words: idolatry, injustice and immorality. Yet even when it was too late for any last-minute show of repentance to prevent exile, the overriding mercy of God was revealed through promises of a return to the land. Isaiah prophesied before and after the fall of Samaria; Jeremiah before the fall of Jerusalem; Ezekiel at that time, and in exile; Daniel (taking the earliest dating), before the return to Jerusalem. Throughout all these prophecies, another strand is woven – one which points to a more wonderful deliverance even than return from exile. This future deliverance would be through a descendant greater than his ancestor, David, and would have world-wide consequences. There are even visions beyond that, of the Last Days and final judgment. We shall pick out the most significant of such prophecies from the major prophetic books, but leave quotations from some of the minor prophets until the chapter on Israel.

Isaiah

In this glorious prophetic book, Isaiah's breadth of vision, including his insights into what we now know to be the far distant future, and his depth of understanding of the nature of God, could only be divinely inspired. The writer alternates between visions of judgment and blessing. He introduces the concept, which is also found in Ezekiel, Joel, Amos and elsewhere, of the Day of the Lord:

> The LORD Almighty has a day in store for all the proud and
>   lofty . . .
> for all the cedars of Lebanon, tall and lofty . . .
> for all the towering mountains and all the high hills,
> for every lofty tower and every fortified wall,
> for every trading ship and every stately vessel.
> The arrogance of man will be brought low and the pride of
>   men humbled;
> the LORD alone will be exalted in that day,
> and the idols will totally disappear. (Isa. 2:12–18)

The Day of the Lord is a never-ending day, beginning with judgment, bringing to an end the days when human beings seem to hold sway, leading to eternity when God is the only Sovereign. It is reinterpreted in the New Testament as the day when Jesus returns. It comes at the end of 'the Last Days', another important prophetic phrase. The NIV Study Bible footnote to Isaiah 2:2 reads: '*the last days*. Can refer to the future generally . . . but usually it seems to have in view the Messianic era. In a real sense the last days began with the first coming of Christ . . . and will be fulfilled at his second coming.' Isaiah had a vision of all nations streaming to the Lord's temple in the Last Days. The word of the Lord would go out from Zion, and nations 'will beat their swords into ploughshares and their spears into pruning hooks' (Isa. 2:2–5).

After these visions about the End Times, the prophet homes in on the disastrous consequences for his own people of their way of life, then looks ahead once more, in one of the most outstanding prophecies about Christ:

> Nevertheless, there will be no more gloom for those who were
> in distress . . . in the future he will honour Galilee of the
> Gentiles, by the way of the sea, along the Jordan. The people

walking in darkness have seen a great light; on those living in the land of the shadow of death a light has dawned. You have enlarged the nation and increased their joy . . . you have shattered the yoke that burdens them . . . the rod of their oppressor . . . For to us a child is born, to us a son is given, and the government will be on his shoulders. And he will be called Wonderful Counsellor, Mighty God, Everlasting Father, Prince of Peace. Of the increase of his government and peace there will be no end. He will reign on David's throne and over his kingdom, establishing and upholding it with justice and righteousness from that time on and for ever. The zeal of the LORD Almighty will accomplish this. (Isa. 9:1–7)

It could be added that the same zeal of the Lord Almighty will ensure that prophecies about Christ's Second Coming will also be fulfilled. A further remarkable prophecy about Christ's first coming and his kingdom, with aspects yet to be fulfilled, is to be found in Isaiah 11:1–9, beginning with these words: 'A shoot will come up from the stump of Jesse [King David's father]; from his roots a Branch will bear fruit. The Spirit of the LORD will rest on him – the Spirit of wisdom and of understanding, the Spirit of counsel and of power, the Spirit of knowledge and of the fear of the LORD.'

Yet more predictions about both judgment and blessing in the Last Days are to be discovered in chapters 24–7, and 34–5. It is significant that arguably the greatest of all the prophets always holds these two aspects in tension when predicting the End Times. God's redemptive purpose through judgment is spelt out in Isaiah 26:9–10: 'When your judgments come upon the earth, the people of the world learn righteousness. Though grace is shown to the wicked, they do not learn righteousness; even in a land of uprightness they go on doing evil and regard not the majesty of the LORD.'

Many scholars attribute chapters 40–66 to another prophet (Deutero-Isaiah). It is in these chapters that the concept of 'the Servant of the Lord' is introduced in the first of four 'Servant Songs' in chapter 42, followed by others in chapters 49, 50 and the most well-known in 52:13–53:12. The Servant embodies

Israel in its ideal form. The ruler Cyrus would deliver the Jews from Babylon, but the Servant would deliver the world from sin, through suffering. It was only after his atoning death that the disciples realised that Jesus perfectly fulfilled these poignant prophecies, uttered so many centuries before his coming. Here is just one extract: 'Surely he took up our infirmities and carried our sorrows, yet we considered him stricken by God, smitten by him, and afflicted. But he was pierced for our transgressions, he was crushed for our iniquities; the punishment that brought us peace was upon him, and by his wounds we are healed' (Isa. 53:4–5)

Those still sceptical of predictive prophecy after studying such scriptures should read a spirited defence of it in Isaiah 48, following chapters about the return from exile in Babylon. The final chapters of the book, 54–66 (bearing in mind that the original was not divided into chapters), include astonishing revelations that Gentiles would also be gathered in by the Lord (56:6–8); that God himself would intervene to deal with sin, by sending a Redeemer, making a covenant with all who repent, involving the work of the Spirit (59:12–21); that this same Spirit of the Sovereign Lord would anoint the Messiah to 'proclaim the year of the LORD's favour and the day of vengeance of our God, to comfort all who mourn' (Isa. 61:2); that after judgment of the enemies of God's people, God will create new heavens and a new earth, where: 'Before they call I will answer; while they are still speaking I will hear. The wolf and the lamb will feed together, and the lion will eat straw like the ox, but dust will be the serpent's food. They will neither harm nor destroy on all my holy mountain' (Isa. 65:24–5).

Jeremiah, Lamentations and Ezekiel

There are far fewer prophecies in *the book of Jeremiah* about the more distant future relative to the time it was written. The prophet was called by God mainly to be a prophet of doom (much against his natural inclination) to Judah, just before its conquest by the Babylonians. There is, however, an intriguing prophecy in chapter 30:4–9 which refers to a terrible time to come some time after the Jews return from captivity:

> These are the words the LORD spoke concerning Israel and
> Judah:
> This is what the LORD says: 'Cries of fear are heard – terror,
> not peace.
> Ask and see: Can a man bear children? Then why do I see
> every strong man with his hands on his stomach like a
> woman in labour, every face turned deathly pale?
> How awful that day will be! None will be like it. It will be a
> time of trouble for Jacob, but he will be saved out of it.
> 'In that day,' declares the LORD Almighty, 'I will break the
> yoke off their necks and will tear off their bonds; no longer
> will foreigners enslave them.
> Instead, they will serve the LORD their God and David their
> king, whom I will raise up for them.'

This time of trouble, sometimes translated distress or tribulation, is referred to again in Daniel 12:1. 'At that time Michael, the great prince who protects your people, will arise. There will be a time of distress such as has not happened from the beginning of nations until then. But at that time your people – everyone whose name is found written in the book – will be delivered.' It is also stressed by Jesus (Matt. 24:21). It is probable that there were preliminary fulfilments in the time of Antiochus Epiphanes (see comments on Daniel) and later when the Roman army surrounded Jerusalem, leading to appalling suffering, but many see a further fulfilment in the Holocaust and one, still future, in the End Times.

In the midst of all this doom and gloom, there are beautiful prophecies of restoration in chapters 30, 31 and 33, including those of salvation by a 'Branch' from David's line (33:15), and God making a new covenant with Israel and Judah. Throughout the books of both Jeremiah and Lamentations (probably also written by the prophet), God's love and grief for his rebellious people are conveyed through his faithful messenger.

The book of Ezekiel is perhaps the most mystifying of all the prophetic books, with strange visions of wheels within wheels at the beginning, the terrifying Gog and Magog in the middle, and a gigantic temple at the end! The wonderfully vivid vision of the

'Valley of Dry Bones' in chapter 37 is easier to understand, as a prophecy of the time when God's people return to the land and to him:

> So I prophesied as I was commanded. And as I was prophesying, there was a noise, a rattling sound, and the bones came together, bone to bone. I looked, and tendons and flesh appeared on them and skin covered them, but there was no breath in them . . . So I prophesied as he commanded me, and breath entered them; they came to life and stood up on their feet – a vast army. . . 'I will put my Spirit in you and you will live, and I will settle you in your own land. Then you will know that I the LORD have spoken, and I have done it, declares the LORD . . . I will make them one nation in the land, on the mountains of Israel. There will be one king over all of them and they will never again be two nations or be divided into two kingdoms . . . and David my servant will be their prince for ever. I will make a covenant of peace with them; it will be an everlasting covenant. I will establish them and increase their numbers, and I will put my sanctuary among them for ever. My dwelling-place will be with them; I will be their God, and they will be my people.'

Most scholars interpret this as being fulfilled in 'the spiritual Israel' – the Church – but we shall point out in our chapter on Israel that some believe in a fulfilment involving the Jewish people as well, which is still to come. Similarly, the horrendous conflict between Gog, Magog and Israel, portrayed in chapter 39, is regarded as either a highly pictorial account of a spiritual battle between God's people and the powers of evil, or a more literal battle, with symbolic detail involving the final revolt of nations after the millennium. The last chapters of Ezekiel are devoted to a vision of a perfect temple, complete with sacrificial system and prince, priests and Levites. A river flows from the temple to the Dead Sea, which begins to teem with life. The land is re-allocated to the twelve tribes, and the holy city, once Yerushalayim (Jerusalem) is renamed Yahweh-Shammah ('The Lord is there'). Those who take this as a prediction yet to be fulfilled literally need to believe in a future temple with walls over three miles long, and a city area of over 3,000 square miles. Most scholars see it as symbolic of the perfect kingdom of God, as seen through Old Testament eyes. The river flowing from the house of God is the water of life, which brings back to life even that which was dead.

Daniel

This fascinating prophetic book is easier to understand, contrary to popular opinion, than some of the others, because it includes a full interpretation of visions in the text. As is the case with many of the prophets, the difficulty for the reader is often more to do with lack of knowledge of history than inability to understand predictions about the future. It is worthwhile trying to acquire even a basic knowledge of Daniel, because it helps to explain many prophetic references in the New Testament.

We shall home straight in on the meaning of Nebuchadnezzar's dream of a large statue – part gold, silver, bronze and iron – which was shattered by a rock. The interpretation is given in Daniel 2:44: 'In the time of those kings, the God of heaven will set up a kingdom that will never be destroyed, nor will it be left to another people. It will crush all those kingdoms and bring them to an end, but it will itself endure for ever.' This means that the last kingdom of iron refers to the Roman Empire, during which Christ announced that the kingdom of God had come. Even those who give the book a very late date (second century BC), some because they cannot believe that God would give such detailed revelations of the future, either have to concede that here is a prediction about the Roman Empire and Christianity, or regard its meaning as referring to an earlier empire, without any satisfactory explanation of the 'rock'.

Other visions and dreams of kings followed, which were interpreted as relevant to their reigns. But the *first* vision which Daniel himself received, described in chapter 7, is of four beasts, which again refer to empires in the present or future from Daniel's perspective, including more detail about the last beast. It had iron teeth and ten horns, but a little horn arose which plucked up three horns, and spoke boastfully. Many take this as referring to Antiochus IV Epiphanes, who during the last few years of his reign (168–164 BC) made a determined effort to destroy the Jewish faith. He in turn foreshadows the even more ruthless 'beast' of the last days, mentioned in the book of Revelation. If, as we believe, it is accepted that a prophecy can have a preliminary and later fulfilment, it is not a problem that only some of the details were fulfilled in the second century BC. This horn (a symbol of power)

> was waging war against the saints and defeating them, until the Ancient of Days came and pronounced judgment in favour of the saints of the Most High, and the time came when they possessed the kingdom . . . Then the sovereignty, power and greatness of the kingdoms under the whole heaven will be handed over to the saints, the people of the Most High. (Dan. 7:21–2, 27)

In the context of the destruction of the beast comes this even more striking prophecy in Daniel 7:13–14, which firmly establishes an end-time context:

> In my vision at night I looked, and there before me was one like a son of man, coming with the clouds of heaven. He approached the Ancient of Days and was led into his presence. He was given authority, glory and sovereign power; all peoples, nations and men of every language worshipped him. His dominion is an everlasting dominion that will not pass away, and his kingdom is one that will never be destroyed.

Jesus claimed the title 'Son of Man', knowing that his fellow Jews would be familiar with the use of this phrase in the book of Daniel (even though that does not exhaust the meaning of the title). In his famous prophetic sermon to his disciples, he enlarged on this reference in Daniel, applying it to his Second Coming (Matt. 24, including verse 30). Since the 'saints' in the prophecy must refer to all the people of God – the Church – at the time of the Second Coming, this vision implies that they will face a very difficult situation of persecution towards the end of the Last

Days. The matter of the ten kingdoms issuing from the Roman kingdom will be discussed in the chapter on Revelation.

Daniel's *second* vision of the ram and goat in chapter 8 has been fulfilled: the animals refer to the Medo-Persian and Grecian kingdoms. The 'horn' here, which started small but grew in power, eventually abolishing sacrifices, is definitely the hated Antiochus. He extended his power over Israel (the Beautiful Land, v. 9), and oppressed godly believers, many of whom died for their faith. He even proclaimed himself to be the equal of God, and brought the sacrificial system to an end. But the army of Judas Maccabeus recaptured Jerusalem, rededicating the temple to the Lord in 164 BC. It is possible to work out how the detailed prediction given in verse 14 was exactly fulfilled.

This prepares us for the *third* vision, a staggering prediction in chapter 9, following Daniel's in-depth intercession, pleading with God to deliver the Jews from exile. 'Seventy "sevens" are decreed for your people and your holy city to finish transgression, to put an end to sin, to atone for wickedness, to bring in everlasting righteousness, to seal up vision and prophecy and to anoint the most holy' (Dan. 9:24). A 'seven' is usually taken to refer to a seven-year period. It is further explained that these 490 years are divided into three periods: 49 years; 434 years; and a final seven-year period. Of these, 483 years are the period from the decree to rebuild Jerusalem, till the coming of the 'Anointed One'. Normally, prophetic numbers are interpreted symbolically, but this appears to be a more exact prediction. Unfortunately, we do not know which was intended of a number of decrees issued in connection with the restoration of Jerusalem; it also looks as if a gap of unspecified length might be envisaged between the 49 and 434 years. We also do not know whether the birth of the Messiah or the beginning of his public ministry is intended – it is probably the latter, the exact date of which is uncertain. The main point is that the Jews of Jesus' day would have known, and the likelihood, as many scholars have computed, that this prediction was exactly fulfilled, makes it an amazing prophecy of the crucifixion – 'the Anointed One will be cut off and will have nothing' (v. 26). Whatever the exact meaning of the numbers, there can be little doubt that the significance of the death of the Messiah is clearly described: 'to finish transgression, to put an end to sin, to atone for wickedness, to bring in everlasting righteousness' (v. 24). It is also made clear that this would be followed by the destruction of Jerusalem and the temple (v. 26), which happened, of course, in AD 70. These fulfilments encourage us to take careful note of the last point – the remaining period of seven years. This is set in the context of the 'end' (vv. 26–7): 'War will continue until the end, and desolations have been decreed. He will confirm a covenant with many for one "seven". In the middle of the "seven" he will put an end to sacrifice and offering. And on a wing he will set up an abomination that causes desolation, until the end that is decreed is poured out on him.' This seems to refer to the activities of the 'end-time beast' referred to in previous prophecies. This subject is expanded in Revelation, where we shall look at it in more detail

The *fourth* vision in chapters 10 and 11 need not concern us here, because it was all fulfilled before the time of Christ. God's purpose in giving it to Daniel must have been to encourage those true to the faith to remain strong in testing times. Its wealth of detail is the main reason why some assign a second-century date (BC) to this book, although others would regard just these two chapters as a later insertion.

The *final* vision in chapter 12 appears to be firmly set in the End Times. There will be a time of distress (tribulation) unequalled since the beginning of nations, but 'everyone whose name is found written in the book' (v. 1) will be delivered. The distinction is clearly made here between those who 'awake: some to everlasting life, others to shame and everlasting contempt'. The chapter closes with further specific time predictions, revolving around what appears to be a three and a half year period until 'the power of the holy people has been finally broken'. Some scholars, basing their views on Daniel, Revelation and elsewhere, think there will be a terrible seven-year period of tribulation in the End Times, in the middle of which it will appear that the power of the Church has been defeated. Admittedly the number seven needs to be treated with caution, as prophetically it often refers to perfection. But, as we have seen in looking at predictions in other chapters, it is clear that numbers in Daniel are not necessarily to be regarded as symbolic.

While fully aware of much of the controversy surrounding this book, our current view is that the majority of the book of Daniel was written before the events predicted, although some of them were to be fulfilled in the near future. Even scholars who cling to a late date are faced with predictions about the Roman Empire and Christ which must have been future to the author, nor should it be forgotten that prophecies from Daniel are taken up by Jesus himself, and elsewhere in the New Testament. Some of those prophecies have been fulfilled in such exact ways that what is predicted about the End Times ought to be taken very seriously. We know that later writers whose works are included in the Apocrypha (which is to be found in some Bibles between the two Testaments) used language similar to, but some of it more exaggerated than, that in Daniel. Basically they used the outward form of 'prophecy' as a teaching method, to encourage their readers about God's faithfulness. What is known of the date of their writings shows they were not true prophets (although they have teaching value), and the distinction between those books and Daniel was recognised by later church councils. The book of Revelation enlarges many of Daniel's themes and was also recognised by the early Church as truly prophetic. Before we turn to that book, from which we can learn more than any other book about the future of the world, the Church and the Jewish people, it is vital that we have some understanding about where Israel fits into God's purposes.

Chapter **7**

Does modern Israel figure in God's future purposes?

'Israel has experienced a hardening in part until the full number of the Gentiles has come in. And so all Israel will be saved.'

(Rom. 11:25–6)

Re-birth of a nation

Israel has rarely been out of the news since its re-birth in 1948, for although geographically it is insignificant, yet surrounded as it is by oil-rich nations, most of which are hostile, it has the potential politically to destabilise the world. At times, it has even looked as though World War III might be triggered by Middle East conflict, centred on Israel. Some of the key questions to be addressed in this chapter are: have any of these developments been prophesied in the Bible? If so, is war or peace in the Middle East predicted for the future? Will there really be an Armageddon? Over and above historical or future developments, what, if anything, is the continuing significance of Israel in God's purposes, especially in the End Times?

There are many unforgettable images in Spielberg's searing film, *Schindler's List*. One is of a little Jewish girl depicted in a bright red coat in an otherwise black–and–white film. In fear she hid under a bed in an attempt to escape from the troops storming the Warsaw ghetto, the last refuge for Polish Jews. Later in the film, her lifeless form, still clothed in the red coat, was seen carelessly tossed on top of a heap of Jewish corpses in a cart.

On the fiftieth anniversary of the birth of modern Israel, the Prime Minister, Benjamin Netanyahu, declared in a speech on 30 April 1998:

> We have our own state. We have our own army and ability to defend ourselves. We are a thriving economy that is fast becoming one of the two or three most technologically advanced societies in the world. We have revived our ancient language. We have reunited our capital. We have done so much. Historians will look back on our achievements and they will ask: 'How did we find this tremendous life force . . . ?' It is nothing short of miraculous. We should all salute it.

But in making clear that his recent visit to the Nazi death camp of Auschwitz had underlined the meaning of the anniversary, he stressed that there was nothing automatic about the remarkable recovery of the Jewish people from the intended death-blow of the Holocaust. He further questioned whether they might not have been lost for ever as a distinct people to all the prevailing forces, including assimilation, were it not for a vital centre to hold them together. It is noteworthy that an article in *The Times* (23 April 1998) about the views of British Jews on the nation of Israel, made abundantly clear that the fact of the existence of Israel has brought a deep sense of security, even to those who have chosen not to live there, in case anything terrible should ever happen to the Jewish people again.

The story of the Jews in the twentieth century is profoundly moving. It was not at all obvious at the beginning of the century that there would ever again be a homeland for the Jewish people in Palestine. Having suffered a devastating defeat by the Romans in AD 70, followed by an unsuccessful attempt to restore an independent state in AD 134, the majority were dispersed, eventually settling in every corner of the globe. Much of their subsequent history in most places was one of restriction, oppression and even terrible persecution, mainly at the hands of the Church, which totally failed to understand the way of Christ in this respect.

The declaration in the Passover ceremony: 'Next year in Jerusalem!' must have seemed a forlorn hope, until Theodor Herzl launched the Zionist movement in Vienna in 1896. It gathered momentum when the movement's headquarters were relocated to London, culminating in the Balfour Declaration in 1917, in which the British Government pledged itself to provide a national homeland for the Jewish people in Palestine, which the League of Nations declared a British Protectorate. But immigration was minimal until the rise to power of Hitler, when tens of thousands of Jews heeded the warning signs, preferring the hardships of life in the mosquito-ridden swamps and harsh wilderness of this tiny little region in the Middle East, to the threat of worse persecution in the relative material comfort of European countries. Sadly, most saw no danger. Even those who did could not have foreseen the depths to which so-called civilised human beings could sink, when Nazi determination to treat the Jews as sub-human developed into a detailed plan of mass extermination.

Even when it was becoming clear after the war that six million had been massacred, the United Nations was divided about providing the Jewish people with a homeland of their own. The British Government, in safeguarding its own interests, had made promises to the Arabs which conflicted with its promises to the Jews, resulting in Holocaust survivors being kept in wretched conditions in camps on Cyprus, pending a decision about their destination. British forces turned back those who tried to escape to Palestine, and in one horrendous episode involving a ship known as *The Exodus* actually returned some pitiful escapees to what had been a concentration camp. It is not difficult to imagine the euphoria of the Jews, when, after a cliff-hanging vote, partition was declared in the United Nations, providing both a Palestinian and a Jewish state. It was only immediately before the vote was taken that the Jewish leaders decided on the name 'Israel'.

The Palestinians

There is another side to the story, which makes it very difficult to answer questions about rightful entitlement to the land. The descendants of the minority of Jews who chose to remain in Palestine in the Roman Empire, even later regaining control of Jerusalem for a brief period (AD 614–17) were eventually conquered by Moslem Arabs in 632, although Islam did not become the majority religion until the thirteenth century. The mixed population of Palestine was never independent, being ruled first from Damascus, then Baghdad, then, after nearly two centuries of Crusader rule, by various dynasties of Mamluk Moslems, who were eventually conquered by the Ottoman Turks in 1516. They were ousted in World War I, by which time the Jews were only 11 per cent of the population. When the UN proposed partition of the land after World War II, trying to do justice to the legitimate claims of both sides, many Arabs and Jews would have been happy to co-exist peacefully, but Arab leaders opposed the plan, convinced that the land belonged to the Palestinian Arabs alone. A further problem was that the partition plan had several glaring defects, including the fact that the new Jewish state would be in three, almost separate, small parcels of land. These indefensible boundaries would have been problematic in any circumstances, not least a hostile atmosphere. But the Jews in their desperate plight felt they had no choice but to accept what was on offer. No sooner had partition been declared than an Arab coalition declared war on the newly born state of Israel. The USA brokered a cease-fire, only for that to be shattered by the Suez Crisis in 1956 and two Arab attacks on Israel in 1967 and 1973. The declared aim was to drive Israel into the sea, regaining Israel for the Palestinians. Against all odds the Arabs were defeated, with the result that Israel's borders were enlarged; over two million Palestinians were absorbed into Arab countries; about a million settled under Israeli military rule in the West Bank and Gaza; 650,000 remained as Israeli citizens in the rest of the country; and a minority, mainly rural labourers who could not find work, had to be looked after through international aid in refugee camps.

In 1970 the PLO, which had become for Palestinians as the Zionist movement was for Jews, modified its stated desire to drive all Jews out of what was Palestine, encouraging instead aspirations for a democratic Palestine in which Palestinians and Jews could have equal rights. It was no surprise that this aim was distrusted and denounced by Israelis. In 1980 Yasser Arafat announced that the new aim of the PLO was to establish an independent state in any land from which the Israelis withdrew, or which the Palestinians 'liberated'. This was further restated as meaning Gaza and the West Bank. Arafat now has administrative control of considerable areas of this territory, but at the time of writing controversy surrounds many West Bank settlements. While many Palestinians continue to nurse their understandable grievances, many Israelis fear that further concessions will lead to indefensible boundaries once again, or even to encroachment on their beloved Jerusalem (although they are fully aware that it is seen as a holy place for Moslems and Christians as well as Jews). Hundreds of thousands on both sides long for peace, but militant Moslems and fanatical Zionists continue to threaten any negotiations.

A divisive subject

The Israel question divides Christians as well. The majority of Christians today have confessed the negative attitudes and actions of previous generations towards Jewish people, and continue to be deeply moved by their past and present sufferings. Nevertheless, there is deep concern about any Jewish discrimination against Palestinians, particularly as God made abundantly clear, through their (Old Testament) Scriptures, that justice and compassion, including for non-Jews in their midst, are a divine imperative for his people. There is a proper Christian and humanitarian concern that international justice needs to be even-handed to both sides. It is recognised that modern Israel is a largely secular state which, like any other, has considerable flaws in its constitution and government; that the views of ultra-orthodox Jews can sometimes be an embarrassment; and that their attempts to discriminate against Christians as well as

Moslems (understandable though that may be) scarcely further harmony.

The views of some Christian Zionists can be rather worrying: their uncritical, even fanatical support for Israel, and their over-literal interpretation of Scripture, which (for instance) leads some to encourage territorial claims about all the land once governed by King Solomon. This would only inflame the present situation, to say the least. Others bring prophecy into disrepute, for example by booking accommodation close to the Mount of Olives, ready to be on the front row in anticipation of the supposed return of Christ there in the year 2000. They have obviously never taken note of the scriptures which make clear that God has revealed to no one the date of Jesus' return. The mayor of Jerusalem suggested setting up tent camps for the six million visitors expected between mid-1999 and the end of the year 2000 – double the usual number of tourists.

Some Christians react to over-literalism by spiritualising all Old Testament prophecies. In fact, there is a widespread 'Replacement Theology', which holds that all the Old Testament prophecies concerning Israel which have not already been literally fulfilled are now to be applied exclusively to the Christian Church. We, on the other hand, believe that many prophecies have a dual reference, to both Israel and the Church. But we recognise that the reasons for the Replacement view warrant serious consideration, particularly in the light of aspects of Jesus' teaching which could appear to lead to that conclusion, as described in the next paragraph.

A spiritual kingdom

When Jesus embarked on his dramatic public ministry, his message was clear: 'The time has come . . . The kingdom of God is near. Repent and believe the good news!' (Mark 1:15). Gradually he taught the crowds and his disciples by word and deed, through parables, sermons, miracles and ultimately by his death, resurrection and sending the Spirit, that the kingdom would be very different from their expectations. It was not just for the Jews (indeed, some would be excluded, or rather, would choose not to belong), but for all who believed he was the Christ, the Son of God, and were prepared to follow him all their lives. Love, as the fulfilment of the law, was to be at the heart of this kingdom. It would begin small, but spread throughout the world, often in unseen ways. There should be no outward trappings of power, in terms of physical boundaries or authoritarian rulers. In fact, Jesus explained: 'The kingdom of God does not come with your careful observation, nor will people say, "Here it is", or "There it is", because the kingdom of God is within you' (Luke 17:20–1). The followers of Jesus would be used to exercise power over sin and demons, but the Holy Spirit, not self, is the source of that power. Ministry to others should be characterised by servanthood, ultimately expressed in self-sacrifice, even to the point of death. Resurrection would follow, for eternal life is in Christ. Jesus said: 'Unless a grain of wheat falls to the ground and dies, it remains only a single seed. But if it dies, it produces many seeds' (John 12:24). The ways of the kingdom turn the values of the world upside down, as the Beatitudes show even more clearly.

No wonder even the disciples were mystified. It is true that they anticipated a kingdom of righteousness and peace where God's Spirit would be poured out in abundance. But the coming kingdom so eagerly awaited by the oppressed Jews, so carefully expounded from the Old Testament by their devout religious teachers, was expected to demonstrate those inner values surrounded by all the outward trappings of power. Yet it is possible with hindsight to see that such a kingdom as Jesus proclaimed, with such a king, was prophesied. Does that mean that all the prophecies as yet unfulfilled, to do with the Jewish people and their land, can be reinterpreted 'spiritually' in connection with the Church and the kingdom of God (which includes the Church, but is a wider concept to do with God's rule in any area of life)? In other words, does the New Testament view of the kingdom of God render obsolete any *special* place for believing Jews, except as members alongside believers of other races, and does it leave behind any claims to particular territory? Those questions can only be answered by looking at New Testament teaching about the Jewish people, and only looking at the relevant Old Testament teaching from that perspective.

A continuing purpose for the Jewish people

It is extremely helpful that St Paul devotes a long section in his epistle to the Romans (chapters 9–11) to address these issues. They were burning questions for the early Church, because it was beginning to dawn on the apostles that the Jewish people as a nation (as opposed to a significant minority of individuals) had not recognised that Jesus was the promised Messiah, let alone the divine Son of God. Yet God had intended that the message of salvation for the world through his Son, who had become incarnate as a Jew, should be proclaimed to humanity by his chosen race, the people of Israel. It is true that the apostles, the disciples and the first converts were Jews, but it was not long before the numbers of Gentile converts began to overtake the number of Jewish believers. Although St Paul was called to be an apostle to the Gentiles, he always took the gospel to the Jews first. He became increasingly distressed when he realised that not only were the majority rejecting his message, but the Church was becoming separated from Judaism, rather than reforming and expanding it.

'Has God rejected his people?' 'Are all the Old Testament promises about the future of the Jewish people null and void?' were vital subjects which have once again become hot issues for Christians in the twentieth century, in connection with the re-establishment of Israel. For Paul, it was not a matter of theoretical discussion – listen to his heart-cry:

> I have great sorrow and unceasing anguish in my heart. For I could wish that I myself were cursed and cut off from Christ for the sake of my brothers, those of my own race, the people of Israel. Theirs is the adoption as sons; theirs the divine glory, the covenants, the receiving of the law, the temple worship and the promises. Theirs are the patriarchs, and from them is traced the human ancestry of Christ, who is God over all, for ever praised! Amen. (Rom. 9:2–5)

He goes on to say that God had not reneged on his promises, which have always been and will only ever be fulfilled through his mercy, in response to faith, not human effort. This means that only some of the Jews will be 'saved', as Paul's quotation from Isaiah chapter 10:22–3 makes clear: 'Isaiah cries out concerning Israel: "Though the number of the Israelites be like the sand by the sea, only the remnant will be saved. For the Lord will carry out his sentence on earth with speed and finality" ' (Rom. 9:27–8). Paul expresses his longing for the salvation of the Israelites: 'For there is no difference between Jew and Gentile – the same Lord is Lord of all and richly blesses all who call on him, for, "Everyone who calls on the name of the Lord will be saved" ' (Rom. 10:12–13). Gentile conversion to Christ would arouse envy in the Jews, as shown by further quotations from Isaiah 65:1–2: ' "I was found by those who did not seek me; I revealed myself to those who did not ask for me." But concerning Israel he says, "All day long I have held out my hands to a disobedient and obstinate people" ' (Rom. 10:20–1).

Then the passage reaches a climax:

Did God reject his people? By no means! . . . God did not reject his people, whom he foreknew . . . Again I ask: Did they stumble so as to fall beyond recovery? Not at all! Rather, because of their transgression, salvation has come to the Gentiles to make Israel envious. But if their transgression means riches for the world, and their loss means riches for the Gentiles, how much greater riches will their fulness bring! (Rom. 11:1–2, 11–12)

Not only has God not abandoned his original chosen people (although only a significant remnant who respond to his way of salvation through Christ will be saved), but *a special time awaits the Jewish people*, it would seem, described as 'fulness'. Commenting on the word 'fulness' Professor F. F. Bruce says, 'the large scale conversion of the Gentile world is to be followed by the large scale conversion of Israel' (*Tyndale Commentary on Romans*, Tyndale Press, 1963, p. 216). That perhaps seems a startling interpretation, until we read more of what Paul goes on to say: 'For if their rejection is the reconciliation of the world, what will their acceptance be but life from the dead?' (11:15).

Clearly the 'rejection' of the Jewish people is temporary (and partial in the sense that a minority of Jewish people have come to faith in Christ). Finally, Paul states clearly:

> I do not want you to be ignorant of this mystery, brothers, so that you may not be conceited: Israel has experienced a hardening in part until the full number of the Gentiles has come in. And so all Israel will be saved, as it is written: 'The deliverer will come from Zion; he will turn godlessness away from Jacob. And this is my covenant with them when I take away their sins.' As far as the gospel is concerned, they are enemies on your account; but as far as election is concerned they are loved on account of the patriarchs, for God's gifts and his call are irrevocable. (11:25–9)

Professor James Dunn states: 'There is now a strong consensus that [all Israel] must mean Israel as a whole, as a people whose corporate identity and wholeness would not be lost even if in the event there were some (or indeed many) individual exceptions' (*World Biblical Commentary*, Word, 1988, vol. 38, p. 138).

We may now ask a very important question. Why have the Jewish people retained their corporate identity for nearly two thousand years since the vast majority lost their country? This, despite the facts that they were not only without a homeland to call their own, but their religious centre (the temple in Jerusalem) has never been rebuilt; their common spoken language of Hebrew fell into disuse until recently; they were obviously affected by assimilation; and there have been both localised and widespread attempts to eliminate them. Under such circumstances, there would normally have been only individuals remaining who would trace their ancestry back to their roots. Could it be that God, the Lord of history, ensured they retained their corporate identity because of his love for them, his choice (election) of them and his irrevocable promises, including the assertion that he has a significant purpose for them as a people, involving large numbers turning to Christ? A passage in Jeremiah chapter 31 (35–40) sheds more light on the subject:

This is what the LORD says, he who appoints the sun to shine by day, who decrees the moon and stars to shine by night, who stirs up the sea so that its waves roar – the LORD Almighty is his name: 'Only if these decrees vanish from my sight,' declares the LORD, 'will the descendants of Israel ever cease to be a nation before me!' This is what the LORD says: 'Only if the heavens above can be measured and the foundations of the earth below be searched out will I reject all the descendants of Israel because of all they have done!' declares the LORD.

The land of Israel in the New Testament

Few Christians disagree that the plain meaning of those chapters in Romans is that one day large numbers of Jewish people (as opposed to small numbers throughout history) will recognise that Jesus is their Messiah, which will result in blessing for the world. It seems this is likely to be in the End Times, because it does not take place 'until the full number of the Gentiles has come in' (11:25), which seems to mean that God will have completed his main purposes for giving the Gentile world an opportunity to respond to the gospel. All this requires a continuing corporate identity for the Jewish people. But that is where widespread agreement ceases. Some Christians believe this presupposes God's continuing purposes for the actual land of Israel, while others see no spiritual significance in the land at all. They would argue that after human beings first sinned, God eventually chose a man (Abraham), then his tribe, then the whole nation of Israelites, to be the recipients and vehicle for the rest of the world of the revelation of his divine nature and purposes. This culminated in sending his Son, Jesus, to bring salvation not only to the Jews but to the rest of the world. The resulting Church was composed of believing Jews and Gentiles, for Jesus broke down any dividing wall of partition. 'There is neither Jew nor Greek, slave nor free, male nor female, for you are all one in Christ Jesus' (Gal. 3:28). However, because the Jewish people as a whole are unresponsive to the gospel, it will require a miracle in the future to bring about their conversion on a wide scale, which could affect Jews wherever they live. But since God's purposes for the salvation of the world long since broadened out beyond one nation, and certainly beyond one geographical area, it would be a retrograde step (so the argument goes) to think that the country of Israel figures in his future purposes. The most that is conceded, in this argument, is that because of the horrendous persecution of the Jews in the last war particularly, God had mercy on them by overruling the counsels of nations, resulting in the provision of something like the pre-1967 allocation of territory for modern Israelis.

This is a compelling argument, which makes it important to see if the New Testament has anything to say about Jewish territory in the future. There is very little, but the few references should not be overlooked. Speaking of the Jewish people Jesus says, 'They will fall by the sword and will be taken as prisoners to all the nations. Jerusalem will be trampled on by the Gentiles until the times of the Gentiles are fulfilled' (Luke 21:24). The first part of this prophecy was fulfilled literally in AD 70, when the Romans destroyed Jerusalem, killing many of the people. The rest were relocated, resulting in the exile of most of their descendants to virtually every nation of the world. It is to be expected, therefore, that the second half of the prophecy will also be fulfilled literally. There is discussion as to the meaning of 'the times of the Gentiles' – some link it with the fulness of the Gentiles referred to earlier – but at the very least it means the period of Gentile domination of Jerusalem, because Jerusalem will be trampled on *until* that time. Is it a coincidence that in 1967 the Jewish people took control of the *whole* of Jerusalem (which had been partitioned after World War II) for the first time (apart from a brief period in the second century AD) in 2,500 years, bearing in mind that before the time of Christ they were subject to other empires? Whatever the rights and wrongs on both sides of the Six Day War, it appears that this prophecy began to be fulfilled then (although some would say that because of Islamic control of what was the temple area, where the Dome of the Rock is situated, the prophecy has not yet been completely fulfilled). The plain and direct implication of Luke 21:24 is that the Jews will re-take control of Jerusalem and this may well be linked with the fulness of the Gentiles coming into the kingdom of God. If so, it does not mean that no more Gentiles would be converted after that, but it does signify God turning his attention to the Jews to bring about the fulfilment of Romans 11:25.

However, it is not sufficient to take one verse like this to establish that the end-times restoration of the Jewish people to Israel is prophesied, and there is very little else on the subject in the New Testament. Before we look at the relevant Old Testament prophecies, it is interesting to note that when the disciples asked Jesus, 'Lord, are you at this time going to restore the kingdom to Israel?' he does not reply negatively but says, 'It is not for you to know the times or dates the Father has set by his own authority' (Acts 1:6–7). Is Jesus implying the kingdom will be restored to Israel but the time is unknown to anyone but God? Some, however, would interpret this verse in a spiritual sense of the word 'kingdom'. Later on in the same chapter (Acts 1:11) it is prophesied that Jesus will return in the same way as the disciples had seen him go. Some believe this means he will return to the Mount of Olives, which brings Jerusalem into prominence again. Is this another indication that the land of Israel is significant in the End Times? Everything depends on how many of the Old Testament prophecies about the land are still relevant today.

Old Testament prophecies about the Promised Land

There are 109 references to the land as given or promised to the Jewish people in the Old Testament. In addition, on thirty-six occasions it states that God swore a solemn oath to give them the land. On a further thirteen occasions the land is promised *'for ever'* (Gen. 13:15; 17:8; 48:4; Exod. 32:13; 1 Chron. 16:15–18; 28:8; 2 Chron. 20:7; Ps. 37:29; Isa. 60:21; Jer. 7:7; 25:5; 33:17–26; Ezek. 37:21–8). So strong is the emphasis that it is clear that the people and the land are very deeply and closely associated. If the two are separated, something is seriously wrong. It is made clear on many occasions that the people will only keep and enjoy the land if they are obedient to God. But although eventually they are exiled for their disobedience, the Lord often assures them that he is willing to forgive and restore them, if they repent. In fact, the Lord is so merciful that although he lays down repentance as the condition of restoration, it seems he does not keep strictly to this. The Jews had already returned to the land after the first exile, before Ezra led them in repentance. It is true that there was a good deal of fasting and lament during the exile to Babylon, and there were genuinely godly individuals among the exiles, such as Daniel, who expressed penitence for the sins of the nation (Dan. 9:1–19). But the Lord said through Zechariah (7:4–7) that much of the fasting of the exiles was insincere. In 458 BC Ezra discovered to his horror that the returned exiles had intermarried with pagan wives, a practice which would almost inevitably lead them into idolatry – the main cause of the exile in the first place. Ezra led them in public repentance (Ezra 9–10). This major repentance, followed by reading the neglected law of God and covenanting to obey it (Neh. 9–10), took place ninety-three years after the first exiles were restored to the land. All of this supports the contention that God in his mercy restored the exiles to the land before there was widespread repentance. At the very best it could be said that there was no more repentance in that exile than there has been in the wider exile in the last 1,900 years. So there is nothing in this area of consideration to rule out the idea that the recent return to Israel is in God's purposes. In fact this could precede the Jewish people turning to Christ, fulfilling Paul's words *'all Israel will be saved'* (Rom. 11:26).

These prophecies do not, however, resolve the problem as to why a parcel of land in the Middle East should have any connection with Jesus' radical teaching about the kingdom of God, which transcends all geographical boundaries. That is why we need to look at other relevant prophecies about the End Times.

Israel and the Last Days

It is important to distinguish prophecies which may well refer to the twentieth-century return to the land from the prophecies (long since fulfilled) of a return from the exile which took place in Old Testament times. In 722 BC Israel (the northern kingdom, which consisted of ten tribes of the people) was exiled to Assyria because of persistent disobedience to God (2 Kgs. 17:6). The exact places of exile mentioned are in present-day NE Syria, Turkey and Iran. There is no evidence that these tribes ever repented and we do not hear of them again. However, in accordance with ancient practice, perhaps some of the ordinary people (agricultural workers) were not exiled but left to care for the land. Archaeology also shows that some of the Israelites from the north fled to Judah during the Assyrian attacks. Then in 586 BC Judah the southern kingdom (consisting of the whole of the tribe of Judah plus parts of Benjamin and Simeon) was exiled to Babylon, again because of persistent rebellion against God. The exiles were taken to what is now Syria and Iraq, which is where ancient Babylon was (although a few fled to Egypt and elsewhere). In 538 BC the exiles began to return from Babylon to Jerusalem. (Later groups returned with Ezra in 458 and Nehemiah in 432.) The countries of these two exiles are to the north or north-east of Israel. Compare this with the return promised from a much wider geographical exile as seen in the following prophecy, which seems clearly to refer to the restoration to Israel which took place in AD 1948. In the context of a chapter prophesying the coming of the Messiah to establish his ultimate rule over the earth, Isaiah states:

> In that day the Lord will reach out his hand a second time to reclaim the remnant that is left of his people from Assyria, from lower Egypt, from upper Egypt, from Cush, from Elam, from Babylonia, from Hamath and from the islands of the sea . . . He will assemble the scattered people of Judah from the four quarters of the earth. (Isa. 11:11–12)

In the book of Joel, there is a prophecy about God summoning all nations for judgment, especially connected with their attitude to Israel. By contrast with Isaiah's prophecy in chapter 2:4 (possibly about heaven or the Millennium), on this occasion the fighting men will beat their ploughshares into swords, and their pruning hooks into spears (Joel 3:10). Joel makes it clear he is describing end-time judgments: 'Multitudes, multitudes in the valley of decision! For the day of the LORD is near in the valley of decision' (3:14). 'The Lord says,

In those days and at that time, when I restore the fortunes of Judah and Jerusalem, I will gather all nations and bring them down to the Valley of Jehoshaphat. There I will enter into judgment against them concerning my inheritance, my people Israel, for they scattered my people among the nations and divided up my land . . . Then you will know that I, the LORD your God, dwell in Zion, my holy hill. Jerusalem will be holy; never again will foreigners invade her . . . Judah will be inhabited for ever and Jerusalem throughout all generations. (Joel 3:1–2, 17, 20)

The prophecy of Amos in chapter 9:14–15 can also only refer to the more recent restoration of Israel: " 'I will bring back my exiled people Israel; they will rebuild the ruined cities and live in them . . . I will plant Israel in their own land, never again to be uprooted from the land I have given them," says the LORD.'

The book of Zechariah, written after the first exile, concludes with an extensive end-time prophecy in connection with Israel and Jerusalem in chapters 12–14. We can do no better than simply quote from this dramatic and moving passage, allowing Scripture to speak for itself.

This is the word of the LORD concerning Israel . . . 'I am going to make Jerusalem a cup that sends all the surrounding peoples reeling. Judah will be besieged as well as Jerusalem. On that day, when all the nations of the earth are gathered against her, I will make Jerusalem an immovable rock for all the nations. All who try to move it will injure themselves . . . On that day I will set out to destroy all the nations that attack Jerusalem. And I will pour out on the house of David and the inhabitants of Jerusalem a spirit of grace and supplication. They will look on me, the one they have pierced, and they will mourn for him as one mourns for an only child, and grieve bitterly for him as one grieves for a firstborn son.' (12:1–2, 9–10)

'On that day a fountain will be opened to the house of David and the inhabitants of Jerusalem, to cleanse them from sin and impurity . . . In the whole land,' declares the LORD, 'two-thirds will be struck down and perish; yet one-third will be left in it. This third I will bring into the fire; I will refine them like silver and test them like gold. They will call on my name and I will answer them; I will say, "They are my people," and they will say, "The LORD is our God." ' (13:1, 8–9)

I will gather all the nations to Jerusalem to fight against it; the city will be captured, the houses ransacked, and the women raped. Half of the city will go into exile, but the rest of the people will not be taken from the city. Then the LORD will go out and fight against those nations, as he fights in the day of battle. On that day his feet will stand on the Mount of Olives, east of Jerusalem, and the Mount of Olives will be split in two from east to west, forming a great valley . . . Then the LORD my God will come, and all the holy ones with him . . . The LORD will be king over the whole earth. On that day there will be one LORD, and his name the only name . . . never again will it be destroyed. Jerusalem will be secure. This is the plague with which the LORD will strike all the nations that fought against Jerusalem: Their flesh will rot while they are still standing on their feet, their eyes will rot in their sockets, and their tongues will rot in their mouths . . . Then the survivors from all the nations that have attacked Jerusalem will go up year after year to worship the King, the LORD Almighty, and to celebrate the Feast of Tabernacles. (14:2–5, 9–10, 12, 16)

A summary of God's purposes for Israel

We have highlighted the following points from Scripture:

1   Even though the kingdom of God is world-wide, and the Church includes believing Jews and Gentiles, God still has a (corporate) future purpose for the Jewish people, whom he chose in love to belong to him, and to whom he made irrevocable promises (Rom. 11).
2   Jesus foretold Jewish control of Jerusalem in the End Times (Luke 21:24).
3   The Old Testament teaches that:

- God swore on oath that he had given the land of Israel to the Jewish people for ever, even though they do not deserve it. (Some Christians would contend that the sin of rejection of the promised Messiah by the Jewish leaders as a whole was so serious that this aspect of God's covenant with the Jewish people became null and void. However, this is not specified in Scripture, but rather appears to be contradicted by Paul's claim that God has not rejected his people.)

- The people and the land are inseparable except in a time of persistent disobedience, but God still promises to restore them.

- Although God judged and exiled the Jews for disobedience, he not only promised restoration to the land conditional on repentance, but actually restored them before they repented after the first exile. It is therefore reasonable to expect that they would be restored to the land a second time, for the promise to be fulfilled that 'all Israel will be saved' (Rom. 11:26).

- In fact, the return of the Jewish people to Israel in the Last Days is foretold.

- It is prophesied that this return would lead to a period of international conflict (Armageddon) in connection with Jerusalem, with devastating consequences for both Israel and all nations. (It is fascinating that this scenario appears so credible in the contemporary international climate. Even so, some commentators spiritualise prophecies such as those in Zechariah, applying them to international persecution of the Church.)

- At this time, there would be widespread repentance concerning the Messiah (but also surely about other corporate sins, such as any injustice towards Palestinians, and breaking God's law in other ways), leading to the salvation of a large 'remnant'.

- These events appear to be connected with the return of Christ.

A connection with the Millennium

The prophecies in Zechariah and elsewhere of massive conflict connected with Jerusalem, interwoven with widespread repentance and restoration of the Jewish people, appear to place these developments immediately prior to the Second Coming. If the establishment of the millennial reign of Jesus is, as argued in a previous chapter, about the revelation of his sovereignty over the nations, it makes wonderful sense of the actual land of Israel and Jerusalem figuring once more in God's purposes. It would be a retrograde step for one country to be elevated above another in the kingdom of God before the return of Christ. But the millennial kingdom, established after his return, seems to be about Jesus being seen to be Lord of this world, before the creation of the new heavens and earth. It therefore could be meaningful to speak about an era when God's kingdom on earth requires an earthly capital, prior to the final rebellion and the destruction of all that is evil. To speak in such seemingly earthly terms is so repugnant to many Christians that they prefer to reinterpret all the points in the previous section, except possibly point 1, as referring to the Church, the kingdom of God and world-wide opposition to God's purposes, etc. Yet even though Jesus massively enlarged any previous understanding of the kingdom, he nowhere spoke of it in ethereal terms. On the contrary, he showed how important it is to God that (for example) justice is brought to bear for the poor and oppressed. He taught us to pray for God's kingdom to come on earth as in heaven. Of course, this means that the Church seeks to further God's will in the world here and now, but in view of the incompleteness of this task, surely God will bring about an answer to the Lord's prayer this side of the new heavens and earth? If he did not do so, he would not be seen to be sovereign of this world system. Believing Jews, Jerusalem and the land of Israel could still have a vital role to fulfil in God's purposes.

However, it is important that Christians learn to respect the integrity of those who hold different views, particularly on the matter of the land of Israel, which, although very important, is not a credal issue. But these subjects are exciting, and if the more literal interpretation is the correct one, unfolding developments which continue to fulfil biblical prophecies could affect the lives of most of the inhabitants of the earth. It is fascinating to read biblical commentaries written before there seemed any likelihood that Israel would ever again be a homeland for the Jewish people. Many take a more literal view of the relevant prophecies, believing against all odds that they would be fulfilled in terms of restoration of the land. For example, William Biederwolf, in *The Prophecy Handbook* (reprinted by World in 1991 *from the 1924 edition*), commenting on Amos 9:15 writes: 'If this, and other prophecies like it, are to be taken literally, then we must look for a literal restoration of the Jews to the land of Palestine sometime in the future, inasmuch as it did not occur in times now past.' Since that came to pass in 1948, commentators would be foolish to be dogmatic that other Old Testament prophecies awaiting fulfilment should not be taken to mean what they say.

We now turn to a New Testament prophetic book which throws more light on this fascinating subject and, in dramatic content, eclipses everything we have considered so far.

Chapter 8

Can Revelation be revealed?

'I looked, and there before me was a door standing open in heaven. And the voice I had first heard speaking to me... said, "Come up here, and I will show you what must take place after this."'

(Rev. 4:1)

Interconnected views

The four horses of the Apocalypse, Armageddon and the beast with ten horns are some of the vivid images from the book of Revelation which have become part of folklore about the end of the world. Yet relatively few have read the book, even though it is so brief (about twenty-five pages long in an average-sized Bible). Most who do are puzzled by it. That is why we shall devote much of this chapter to retelling the visions portrayed, with comments of explanation where necessary. Inevitably this will reveal something of our own current understanding and interpretation of this last book of the Bible. But we are trying to work out the same principles of prophecy which we have already taught (multiple reference; concertina effect; dual aspect and an emphasis on purpose), which in effect hold together some of the hundreds of different interpretations. The next section will be devoted to mentioning briefly the four main schools of thought, before we dip into the pages of one of the most thrilling books ever written.

The historicist view is that Revelation is mainly about the entire church age between the first and second comings of Jesus. Some who hold this view believe that it begins with events contemporary to the author and proceeds in a linear way, describing history as it unfolds after that (some events, therefore, have not yet taken place). A variation on this view is that it deals with the whole of history more than once, in a cyclical way, from different perspectives.

The futurist view is that the book is about the end of the End Times – the events immediately preceding and following the Second Coming of Christ.

The preterist view (from the word 'preterite', meaning 'past') is that the book is about history which is in the distant past from a modern perspective. Some believe it is about the time contemporary to the writer, which has led to various theses about which particular emperor was Caesar at the time of writing (for example, Nero or, more likely, Domitian). According to that theory, the book is not predictive at all. A variant on the preterist view is that St John was predicting the relatively near future – the various persecutions which would befall the Church in the Roman Empire, before the conversion of Constantine.

The idealist view is that Revelation was not written to predict future events, but depicts the age-long struggle between good and evil, God and the devil. Emphasis is placed on the vital lessons which Christians should learn from this book, including the importance of enduring and overcoming trials in the light of the celebration in heaven of Christ's victory over evil. The more liberal version of this view goes so far as to assert that there will be no Second Coming, no end to the world. All end-time prophecies are spiritualised as being about lessons to be learned for the Church and each individual believer.

We would want to affirm that it is possible to hold together many of these views, although there is no space in one chapter to go into details as to how this may be achieved. One could describe this as *the comprehensivist view*. In this paragraph, we simply provide a glimpse of how one could read Revelation, bearing the four main views in mind. We shall later illustrate in more detail when looking at chapter 13. In general terms, there is no question that many events pictured recur throughout history, at different times, in various parts of the world, as maintained in the historicist view. One could imagine a believer today, who is being persecuted for the Faith (for example in China or militant Islamic regimes), drawing enormous comfort from discovering parallels to contemporary experience, and being given strength to endure. As regards the futurist view, there are, for example, many references to the return of Christ, with its immediate prelude and aftermath. In fact, one would have to distort the text to deny relevance to that defining time in future world history. It is also entirely possible to decode Revelation according to the preterist view, recognising detailed relevance to the time of one or other persecuting Caesar, or trials throughout the pre-christianised Roman Empire, at or after the time of authorship. The idealist view also helps the reader to understand that the prophetic packaging contains a vital message, although it must be obvious that we would strongly contest the version which spiritualises away all predictive significance. However, all may agree that there are important lessons which Christians should learn from this book, especially that belief in the sovereign power of God makes it possible to overcome, even in the most testing circumstances. It is essential to be reminded that St John was writing at a time when the very survival of Christianity was threatened. If early believers had not heeded the challenge to be overcomers, it is sobering to realise that the early Church might have disappeared without trace.

For two hundred years, the pressure on Christians to conform to the beliefs and standards of their world was intense. Thousands – ultimately millions – of believers faced the prospect of, or actually suffered, discrimination, deprivation, vilification, physical persecution and, in many cases, martyrdom. Dr H. B. Workman, in his book *Persecution in the Early Church* (Wyvern Books, The Epworth Press, 1960, p. 131), attempted to confine his account to strictly historical cases, while admitting, too, that in part some of the punishments were normal judicial processes of that age. He wrote of Christian martyrdoms:

Some . . . were shut up in a sack with snakes and thrown into the sea; others were tied to huge stones and cast into a river. For Christians the cross itself was not deemed sufficient agony; hanging on the tree, they were beaten with rods . . . Christians were tied to catapults, and so wrenched limb from limb. Some, like Ignatius, were thrown to the beasts; others tied to their horns. Women were stripped, enclosed in nets, and exposed to the attacks of furious bulls . . . Not a few were broken on the wheel . . . Of some the feet were slowly burned away, cold water being poured over them the while lest the victims should expire too rapidly.

The blood of the martyrs was indeed the seed of the Church. Christians worshipping in a more tolerant climate of opinion are for ever indebted to them, and to all who have suffered, or are still suffering, for Christ. The writer of Revelation, the apostle John, understood such suffering, having been exiled to the island of Patmos 'because of the word of God and the testimony of Jesus' (Rev. 1:9). He wrote from personal experience.

Vantage point of heaven

It is impossible to understand the book of Revelation unless attention is paid to John's perspective. From chapter 4, he sees his visions of both heaven and earth from a privileged position, in the throne-room of heaven. This explains why events on earth seem so horrific, by contrast with the glory of heaven. Prior to receiving the invitation to 'Come up here' (4:1), John has a vision of the Person who is the main subject of the Revelation (chapter 1), and receives messages to convey to seven churches on the mainland of Asia Minor (chapters 2–3).

At the beginning of the book, the author immediately sets out its purpose: it is a prophecy, designed to show Christians 'what must soon take place' (1:1, 3). 'Soon' is seen from the perspective of the reader today to be an elastic term, because it is not long before John refers to the Second Coming, which he relates to the poignant prophecy in Zechariah, referred to in the previous chapter: 'Look, he is coming with the clouds, and every eye will see him, even those who pierced him; and all the peoples of the earth will mourn because of him. So shall it be! Amen' (1:7).

The description which follows of the Lord God Almighty, as 'the Alpha and the Omega . . . who is, and who was, and who is to come' (1:8) is shortly after applied to Jesus, in verse 17 and in 22:13, leaving us in no doubt that John regarded him as on a par with God the Father, and that history, past, present and future, is under his control. It is 'his story', which is why prophecy is possible. The very person who bestrides history, around whom not only the human story but the universe revolves, is the one who speaks to the prophets, including John. The book is no less than the Revelation of Jesus Christ (1:1, 17–19), who is seen in awesome glory (1:12–16). He is the risen, ascended, reigning, almighty Lord, who commands John to write 'what you have seen, what is now and what will take place later' (1:19).

After being given messages (to which we cannot devote space here) to encourage, warn, challenge and predict persecution in the near future for seven churches (chapters 2–3), the apostle finds himself in the Spirit in heaven. From that point on he has astounding visions, which swing violently between observing the glorious worship in heaven and the terrible events on earth as seen from a heavenly vantage point. It is made plain to John straight away that he is to glimpse events still future (4:1).

Horrors on earth

It is when the seals of a scroll in the right hand of God are opened that horrors are unleashed on earth. But first, there is a problem. Who is worthy to break the seals and open the scroll? Neither the exalted angelic creatures who lead the unceasing worship to the Lord God, nor the twenty-four elders (probably representing the twelve tribes of Israel and the twelve apostles, thus uniting believing Israel and the Church in one worshipping community) are found to be worthy. No one is worthy, until Jesus has triumphed (5:5). He is revealed as both Lion and Lamb: the Messianic ruler predicted as long ago as in the book of Genesis (49:8–10), and the suffering Saviour of the world. The same Person who died to purchase people for God 'from every tribe

and language and people and nation . . . to serve our God, and . . .
reign on the earth' (Rev. 5:9–10), who is regarded as worthy 'to
receive power and wealth and wisdom and strength and honour
and glory and praise' (5:12), is the only One fit to open the scroll
of God. As he takes it, the worship of heaven is directed to the
Lamb.

It must have come as a dreadful shock to John to be shown
visions of the contents of the scroll. This Jesus, whom he had
glimpsed in glory, was giving the signal, as it were, for terrible
events to unfold on the earth. This was the same Christ who had
healed the sick, comforted the oppressed, and had suffered an
agonising death for the salvation of the world. Such a seeming
contradiction cannot be understood, unless it is realised first
that Jesus is Judge as well as Saviour. Second, he does not cause
the events, but rather demonstrates his sovereignty over all the
events of history and their timing. As we shall see, some of these
events have recurred throughout history, including before the
time of Christ. This underlines the point that Jesus is the Alpha
and Omega: the Beginning and the End.

The four horses of the Apocalypse (another word for
Revelation) now make their fearsome appearance (6:2–8): the
white, red, black and pale horses are given power, respectively,
to unleash conquest, war, economic deprivation (within limits)
and death. As a result of their activities, a quarter of the
population of the world die by sword, famine, plague and also
wild beasts. It is understandable that, at various times in history,
horrendous events have been directly related there and then to
the judgments in Revelation. For example, when the Black Death
eliminated one-third of the population of Europe in the
fourteenth century, it must have seemed that not only had the
seals been opened, but the world was coming to an end. This
also applies in times of persecution: the opening of the fifth seal
of the scroll reveals martyrs for the Faith waiting to be vindicated.
The sixth leads to a massive earthquake, the results of which are
described in terms of cosmic disturbance, the removal of
mountains and islands, and universal terror when confronted
by the wrath of the Lamb. The similarity of the 'seal judgments'
to the prophecies of Jesus (in the synoptic gospels) is striking. It

is clear that, whatever relevance there might be, whether future or contemporary to the writer, such tragedies also occur throughout history – although the last event, described in terms of an earthquake to end all earthquakes (6:12–17), *may* point to a future cataclysmic event, connected with end-time judgment.

John is on a unique roller-coaster ride, which fills him with horror as he swoops down to view the unfolding tragedy of human history, only to be once more on top of the world, entering into something of the glory of heaven. So it is that (as described in chapter 7), having been reassured there is protection in the Last Days for the people of Israel who are believers, he witnesses the praises of an innumerable multi-ethnic multitude, overflowing with thankfulness to God and the Lamb for their salvation. Some scholars see these as believers down through the ages who have overcome by faith in the difficulties of life, whereas others regard them as those who triumph in a particular period – 'the great tribulation' (7:14) – of the End Times.

The opening of the seventh seal leads to further horrors, this time announced by seven angels, each blowing a trumpet. (The 'seal' judgments in chapter 6 give way to the 'trumpet' judgments in chapters 7–8, which in turn lead on to the 'bowl' judgments in chapter 16). The ruination resulting from the trumpet judgments affects a third of the earth. Even the otherwise unceasing worship of heaven falls silent for half an hour, in anticipation of what is to come (8:1). The contrast becomes even more apparent between the perfection of heaven, and the sickening devastation of the earth, largely described this time in terms of natural disasters. No part of creation remains unaffected: the land, the sea, the rivers, the skies, and the life sustained by these elements. Prior to relatively recent discoveries about how human activities have polluted the environment, possibly damaging the ecology beyond repair, it could have been thought that all these disasters were direct 'acts of God'. We now know better – most of these 'judgments' are in fact God allowing the consequences of human sin, whether perpetrated wittingly or unwittingly, to take their course. Worse was to come in John's visions.

Invasion from the Abyss

The terminology used from chapter 9 becomes increasingly apocalyptic. In other words, extreme, vivid imagery is used to attempt to describe the indescribable. John searched for words to convey his terrifying visions, only occasionally giving any interpretation to the reader, much as is the case if anyone attempts to describe a nightmare. The reason for these increasingly lurid visions soon becomes apparent. Having shown John something of the damage caused to planet Earth and its inhabitants by human sin and natural disasters, the Spirit now reveals glimpses of the interaction of the devil and his minions with humanity. It is fascinating that the seal visions major on problems directly caused by human sin (such as war) but move on to 'natural disasters' (many still caused by human sin), which then become the focus of the trumpet visions. As these unfold, the focus moves to what is taking place in the kingdom of darkness (or the Abyss, as it is described in chapter 9), and the effect of its power over human beings, except for those who belong to God. The only encouragements are that God is seen to be sovereign over how far demonic forces are allowed to hold sway (9:4, 5, 10), and he protects those who belong to him.

Locusts now make their appearance – yet unlike any known to humanity (9:7–10). They prove to be demonic forces from the pit of hell, who wreak havoc on the earth. At first they appear deceptively beautiful, but they are also very powerful, and have a harmful sting in the tail. This is usually the way the devil presents temptation to sin, including occult involvement. Four angels of death are then released, who have forces at their disposal numbering two hundred million (9:16), signifying legions of demons. Abaddon, or Apollyon, is their king. These are names for the devil, meaning destruction (9:11). He might sometimes appear as an angel of light, but his true nature is the antithesis of God's character: personification of hatred, as opposed to love; destroyer, as opposed to creator. He is not omnipotent, but is able to exercise influence anywhere in the world through his hosts of 'fallen' angels. He can only gain power over people as a result of sin – idolatry, immorality, murder, theft and 'magic arts' are specified in verses 20–21. But even though the destructive consequences of such behaviour are obvious, there is no widespread repentance.

The two witnesses

The unfolding drama of Revelation moves into another dimension from chapter 10 onwards. Hitherto, John has been viewing many of the on-going traumas suffered by humankind as a result of human sin, aided and abetted by demonic activity. He has been appalled by the contrast between the suffering on earth, resulting from disobedience to God, and the awe-inspiring worship in heaven, where God's will is fulfilled. But before the seventh trumpet is sounded, it is made clear to the reader that visions from this point on are in connection with the traumatic developments surrounding the transition from the state of affairs just described to God's will being done on earth as in heaven. In other words, the book now begins to refer to the last of the Last Days (while still having some historic and on-going reference):

> Then I saw another mighty angel coming down from heaven. He was robed in a cloud, with a rainbow above his head; his face was like the sun, and his legs were like fiery pillars . . . Then the angel I had seen standing on the sea and on the land raised his right hand to heaven. And he swore by him who lives for ever and ever, who created the heavens and all that is in them, the earth and all that is in it, and the sea and all that is in it, and said, 'There will be no more delay! But in the days when the seventh angel is about to sound his trumpet, the mystery of God will be accomplished, just as he announced to his servants the prophets.' (Rev. 10:1–7)

At this point John takes the scroll, which is about prophesying to 'many peoples, nations, languages and kings' (v. 11). What might seem to be a great privilege turns into a bitter duty (10:9–11). Far from witnessing unmitigated glory connected with the return of Jesus, John was to see just how fiercely the devil would contest the fulfilment of the kingdom of God – through widespread deceit, unbridled revelation of evil and a final attempt to exterminate the people of God. Just before and after the dreaded seventh trumpet is blown, revealing two terrifying beasts, John is given two visions, one of two witnesses and the other of a woman and a dragon. These are the two aspects of Revelation which are perhaps the most difficult to interpret. The two witnesses (variously described as olive trees or lampstands) prophesy for forty-two months, before being attacked and killed by the 'beast from the Abyss' (who is later described in more detail), only to rise again and be taken into heaven in a cloud. At this point, the severe earthquake (previously mentioned) takes place. There are various theories about the two witnesses, but we prefer the interpretation in which the two witnesses are taken as referring to the Church and the remnant of Israel who turn to the Messiah in the Last Days. The period of time specified refers to the first half of the final period of seven years (mentioned in Daniel chapter 9). It had come to symbolise the period of the final demonic onslaught against God's people, before the return of Jesus. Those who think they have succeeded in destroying the children of God are astonished when they rise again. This would seem to refer to the time when they are taken up to be with the Lord for ever, at the Second Coming. The following verse appears to confirm that view: 'The seventh angel sounded his trumpet, and there were loud voices in heaven, which said: "The kingdom of the world has become the kingdom of our Lord and of his Christ, and he will reign for ever and ever" ' (Rev. 11:15). It would seem that John is given this glimpse of final victory before further details are revealed of horrors to come.

The woman and child

The vision of the woman who gives birth to a male child, whom Satan attempts to destroy, may well reinforce the vision of the two witnesses. We do not think it refers to Mary and Jesus, because he was not 'snatched up to God' (12:5) as a child. It is not possible here to go into different interpretations, other than to draw attention to an interesting futurist view: that the woman 'clothed with the sun, with the moon under her feet and a crown of twelve stars on her head' refers to the Church in the Last Days, which 'gives birth', so to speak, to believing Jews. There have, of course, been a minority of Jewish believers throughout history, who are united with believing Gentiles in the universal Church. But, as we have seen when looking at Romans 9–11, a time is prophesied when a *large* minority, or 'remnant', of Israel will be saved. This will be partly through the witness of the mainly Gentile Church (although it is important to remember that the Church first came into being through the witness of the apostles, all of whom were Jews). It is worth noting that, in Scripture, the Church is usually referred to in the feminine, and Israel in the masculine. The dragon (Satan) immediately tries to destroy the male child – this newly formed company of Jewish believers, for whom God has a special purpose. That is revealed as being to 'rule all the nations with an iron sceptre' (presumably in the Millennium). The child is snatched up to God, and the woman is protected by God 'in the desert'. This would seem to imply the martyrdom of many believing Jews, and the virtual disappearance of the Church in any organised form. Far from the Church being raptured either before or halfway through the final persecution, its disappearance may well mean that the organised Church world-wide has been forced to disband. This has been the case in many situations of persecution throughout history (e.g. in Albania prior to the collapse of Communism). Such examples are a foretaste of the last persecution. Human governments may think they have liquidated the Church: for example, Jiang Qing, wife of Chairman Mao, said in the middle of the Cultural Revolution, 'Christianity in China has already been put into a museum. There are no more believers.' But the devil knows better. He realises that the Church has merely been driven underground and might even be thriving in her suffering (as is the case in China today, despite continuing persecution), so in his fury he turns his attention to individual believers: 'Then the dragon was enraged at the woman and went off to make war against the rest of her offspring – those who obey God's commandments and hold to the testimony of Jesus' (Rev. 12:17).

The unholy trinity

It is possible to illustrate clearly from chapter 13 how the four main views of Revelation may be applied, in order to understand the full meaning of the vision. What follows is the text of the chapter, edited for brevity:

> And the dragon stood on the shore of the sea. And I saw a beast coming out of the sea. He had ten horns and seven heads . . . The dragon gave the beast . . . great authority. One of the heads of the beast seemed to have had a fatal wound, but the fatal wound had been healed. The whole world was astonished and followed the beast. Men worshipped the dragon . . . and they also worshipped the beast . . . The beast was given a mouth to utter proud words and blasphemies and to exercise his authority for forty-two months. He was given power to make war against the saints and to conquer them. And he was given authority over every tribe, people, language and nation. All inhabitants of the earth will worship the beast – all whose names have not been written in the book of life belonging to the Lamb that was slain from the creation of the world . . . Then I saw another beast, coming out of the earth. He had two horns like a lamb, but he spoke like a dragon. He exercised all the authority of the first beast on his behalf, and made the earth and its inhabitants worship the first beast, whose fatal wound had been healed. And he performed great and miraculous signs [which] deceived the inhabitants of the earth . . . He also forced everyone, small and great, rich and poor, free and slave, to receive a mark on his right hand or on his forehead, so that no one could buy or sell unless he had the mark, which is the name of the beast or the number of his name. This calls for wisdom. If anyone has insight, let him calculate the number of the beast, for it is man's number. His number is 666.

According to the *preterist* view, there is much in this passage which can be directly related to times of persecution by one or more Roman emperors. For example, the first Caesar to persecute

Christians was the notorious Nero. His name, if written in Hebrew, adds up to 666, because letters of the alphabet were used to represent numbers. Rumours persisted for decades that he had never really died, but would come back to terrorise the empire. There is also much, according to the *historicist* view, which can be applied throughout history when dictators such as Napoleon or Hitler have attempted world domination, or more particularly when the Soviet Union attempted world rule combined with religious persecution, including that of Christians. Regarding the combination with economic oppression, many Christians have been victims of job discrimination, for example, or other forms of economic hardship, in situations of persecution. Many who are too wedded to the world compromise under such pressure. According to the *idealist* view, the main emphasis is on the timeless message of Revelation, which is not to engender fear but to encourage patient endurance, faith, hope and love, claiming the victory of Jesus in all circumstances. But what of the *futurist* view? In particular, does this passage tell us anything about the end of the End Times?

According to the futurist view, there can be no doubt that what is described in the second half of Revelation is a final manifestation of evil immediately prior to the return of Christ. This takes the form of an unholy trinitarian alliance between secular and pseudo-religious powers, manipulated by demonic forces. There are two 'beasts': the first beast arises from 'the Abyss' (17:8), and the second beast is referred to elsewhere as the false prophet (19:20). They seem to be a counterfeit trinity, the father-figure being Satan himself. In chapter 17 more details are supplied about the beast:

Then the angel said to me: 'Why are you astonished? I will explain to you the mystery of . . . the beast . . . which has the seven heads and ten horns. The beast, which you saw, once was, now is not, and will come up out of the Abyss and go to his destruction . . . This calls for a mind with wisdom. The seven heads are seven hills . . . They are also seven kings . . . The beast who once was, and now is not, is an eighth king. He belongs to the seven and is going to his destruction. The ten horns you saw are ten kings who have not yet received a kingdom, but who for one hour will receive authority as kings along with the beast . . . They will make war against the Lamb, but the Lamb will overcome them because he is Lord of lords and King of kings – and with him will be his called, chosen and faithful followers. (Rev. 17:7–14)

The seven hills was a normal way of alluding to Rome (because it was originally built on seven hills), and the seven kings could initially have referred to emperors, or have been symbolic of the Roman Empire. (There are obvious references to some of Daniel's visions here, including Daniel 7:14–28.) The beast, as the eighth king, is therefore in some sense connected to Rome. There may have been an initial and partial historical fulfilment, but the final fulfilment, according to the futurist view, has not yet taken place (because the destruction of the beast is linked elsewhere with end-time events). It is because of the link with Rome that some interpreters have demonised the office of the Pope; whereas others have seen relevance to the European Community (in the belief that it will ultimately consist of ten member-nations), because of the geographical connection with the Roman Empire. There is, however, another interpretation.

A counterfeit New World Order?

At this point we shall describe in detail one particular futurist interpretation, because it is widely held in some church circles, and its outworking in the future is entirely plausible. After that, we shall utter a word of caution. In this view, the unholy trinity will attempt to inaugurate a New World Order which would be the demonic counterfeit of, and an attempt to pre-empt, the full manifestation of the kingdom of God. It is not, of course, inconceivable that there could be an attempt in the twenty-first century to inaugurate a universal economic union, which would obviously have dominant international power. President Bush first publicised the phrase 'New World Order' in connection with the international alliance forged in the Gulf War at the beginning of the last decade of the twentieth century. Boris Yeltsin told the

UN in 1992 that 'the time has come to consider creating a global system for the protection of the world community'. While there is political fragmentation at national level in many countries, there is increasing acceptance that no nation can go it alone economically, and growing recognition that complex problems can only be resolved at international level. Some claim there is evidence of plans to divide the world into ten politico/economic units (the ten kings who will exercise short-lived authority alongside the beast?). The link with Rome in the biblical description could have various explanations. One is that the EC could possibly be the dominant, or at least the first experimental unit, of the world government.

It is not difficult to imagine the awesome power of such a world system, bearing in mind that absolute power corrupts absolutely. At first much good could be achieved, with seeming miracles being displayed, such as successful efforts to feed the hungry millions. If this system were to be run by a world leader, one could imagine the adulation which would ensue – but totalitarian evil would soon be unleashed. Since monotheistic religions could be thought to stand in the way of world peace, persecution of their adherents is inevitable. This could begin with economic sanctions against all who refuse to worship the beast. We shall not attempt to outline the scores of differing interpretations of the mark of the beast on the right hand or forehead (13:16), except that those who hold certain views need to add a rider that believers do not need to fear that they could be caught unawares. The utterly evil nature of the leaders of the New World Order would eventually become obvious, and resistance to any worship connected with them would be essential for Christians.

Futurists assert that it would be foolish, in the present climate, for anyone to maintain that an attempt to create a New World Order is an impossibility, even though it would probably be short-lived (because such a demonstration of absolute power is almost bound to implode). They maintain that the devil is highly likely to attempt one final manifestation – even an incarnation – of himself, whether through a powerful leader, or group, or government. Many also see a connection between the living image which all have to worship (Rev. 13:14–15) and the 'abomination that causes desolation' which Jesus (quoting from Daniel 9:27) prophesied would herald widespread deceit and distress immediately prior to his return (Matt. 24:15–21).

We want to utter three warnings about this futurist interpretation, apart from the obvious one that Christians have been convinced in the past that a certain scenario would be the fulfilment of these prophecies, only to be proved wrong. One is that Christians should not live in fear of such possibilities or, even worse, scan every development in current events almost with a kind of twisted hope that they will see their interpretation coming to pass. The second caution is that, just supposing such a scenario were to begin to unfold, it would be quite wrong for Christians to oppose positive developments – particularly international plans for peace or famine relief, etc., through fear that the next step might be evidence that the antichrist is behind such progress. Any such opposition would be not only ridiculous but sinful, unless and until some obvious unethical or idolatrous link became clear (e.g. economic help only being made available to certain racial groups, or to those who compromise their faith). Third, developments in the End Times are highly likely to transcend all expectations, in connection with the kingdom of darkness as well as the kingdom of God. The exact fulfilment of these prophecies remains a mystery, but certainly one would expect all hell to be let loose prior to the return of Jesus. This is, after all, the devil's last chance to retain any control over the earth, while seeking even to prevent the Second Coming, leading as it will to the full manifestation of the kingdom of God on this earth (whether in the Millennium or the new earth). But if believers get locked into one particular interpretation, it is possible they might miss the reality, which might be more subtle than they have imagined.

Two harvests

After such a fearful vision, it brings sweet sorrow to John to see in heaven those believers who have been offered as firstfruits to God (14:1–5). They have probably been martyred for their faith in circumstances such as those described above. An angel is sent to facilitate the last opportunity for the gospel to be proclaimed to the whole earth (14:6-7) which leads to the Son of Man reaping the harvest (probably of believers) before another angel gives the order for a final harvest of judgment (to be described in chapters 16–18), which completes God's wrath (14:14–15:1). It sounds strange to our ears that both aspects of the harvest are a cue for further worship in heaven. Strange, that is, unless we recognise how important salvation and justice are to God:

> Great and marvellous are your deeds, Lord God Almighty.
> Just and true are your ways, King of the ages.
> Who will not fear you, O Lord, and bring glory to your name?
> For you alone are holy. All nations will come and worship before you,
> for your righteous acts have been revealed. (Rev. 15:3–4)

Seven bowls of wrath

The final judgments are now described in more detail: seven bowls poured out on humanity, containing plagues of boils afflicting worshippers of the beast; the sea turning to blood, this time causing death to all its living creatures; the same happening to the rivers and springs; scorching temperatures for the inhabitants of the earth. These four are reminiscent of the seal judgments, except their destructive power is more total. Those who take them at their face value point out that abuse of God's creation by human beings ultimately is bound to harm the abusers – whether through plagues for which there is no cure, due to over-use of antibiotics in the food chain, giving rise to resistant super-bugs; or pollution of water supplies; or global warming resulting from emissions inimical to the earth's atmosphere. Then the kingdom of the beast is plunged into darkness (perhaps referring to the time when the evil nature of his regime is revealed) but still there is no repentance. When the sixth bowl is poured out, the kings of the whole world gather for battle at Armageddon; and finally the last great earthquake (possibly a metaphor, or a terrible disaster) is described once more. It is noteworthy that the Second Coming of Jesus is mentioned in the middle of the reference to Armageddon (16:15). The destruction of 'Babylon' (explained in the next paragraph) is mentioned, then described in more detail in chapters 17 and 18. It should be no surprise that all hell is let loose immediately before the Second Coming.

The end of the present world order

John now sees a startling vision of a prostitute, described in another way as Babylon. It is quite clear from the text what this means: 'The woman you saw is the great city that rules over the kings of the earth' (17:18). It is important to understand that ever since the Jews were conquered by the Babylonians, Babylon came to symbolise the antithesis of all that Jerusalem represented. Jerusalem witnessed to the rule of the one true God, whereas Babylon was a testimony to the rule of man in opposition to the will of God. The prostitute is the (demonic) power behind all corrupted by government, who become intoxicated by power and material gain, particularly at the expense of those they oppress, including 'the saints' (17:6). It is fascinating to note that the beast comes to power in close co-operation with corrupt governments (the prostitute rides the beast), but is responsible for bringing about the destruction of that corrupt world order, to inaugurate an even more evil regime (17:16–17). This time it is one that is totally, rather than partially, demonised. According to some interpretations, this may describe a scenario in which the financial systems which shore up international economy and national government are brought to a state of collapse, leading to terrible panic world-wide (and, some believe, to the need for world government). The interconnectedness of world finances, including via modern technology, is believed to render such a situation a credible possibility. In *The Times* on 18 June 1998, there was this front-page headline: 'US goes to rescue of plunging yen'. Here are quotations from the article:

> President Clinton . . . launched a $2 billion rescue operation to shore up the plummeting Japanese yen and prevent a

dramatic worsening of the Asian financial crisis that could trigger a world slump. The move marked America's acceptance that it must act as the world's financial policeman, as the sole power capable of tackling the threats posed by the previously glittering Asian economies . . . Earlier this week, China said that the collapse of the yen could force it to devalue its own currency, the yuan, which could in turn trigger another collapse in Asian currencies . . . And on Tuesday, a leading World Bank official gave warning that Asia was on the threshold of depression that threatened a global economic slump.

What follows in chapter 18 is a powerful lament over the fall of Babylon, from which we take brief extracts:

'Fallen! Fallen is Babylon the Great! She has become a home for demons and a haunt for every evil spirit . . . For all the nations have drunk the maddening wine of her adulteries. The kings of the earth committed adultery with her, and the merchants of the earth grew rich from her excessive luxuries.' Then I heard another voice from heaven say: 'Come out of her, my people, so that you will not share in her sins . . . for . . . God has remembered her crimes . . . The merchants of the earth will weep and mourn over her because no one buys their cargoes any more – cargoes of gold, silver, precious stones and pearls; fine linen, purple, silk . . . costly wood . . . and marble; cargoes of . . . wine and olive oil, of fine flour and wheat; cattle and sheep . . . and bodies and souls of men . . .' Then a mighty angel picked up a boulder . . . and threw it into the sea, and said: 'With such violence the great city of Babylon will be thrown down, never to be found again . . . No workman of any trade will ever be found in you again . . . The voice of bridegroom and bride will never be heard in you again. Your merchants were the world's great men. By your magic spell all the nations were led astray. In her was found the blood of prophets and of the saints, and of all who have been killed on the earth.'

Armageddon and the Millennium

A chorus of hallelujahs is heard in heaven at this point, celebrating the true judgments of God, his sovereignty over the affairs of humanity, and the near approach of the wedding of the Lamb. Jesus will be united more completely with his Church than was possible while the Church was tainted with impurities. This section (19:1–10) closes with the interesting comment: 'For the testimony of Jesus is the spirit of prophecy.' This could well be a reminder that true Spirit-inspired prophecy ultimately testifies about Jesus.

This same Jesus, described in terms of a bridegroom, is now depicted as the rider on a white horse, charging out of heaven to defeat the combined armies of the earth arrayed against him (and against the Church). He is named as 'the Word of God' (19:13), and 'King of kings and Lord of lords' (19:16). Many interpreters see this as a vivid description of the Second Coming. In the massive conflict at this time between the powers of good and evil (described in 16:16 as Armageddon) defeat of the opposition is total, including that of the dreaded beast and false prophet. Their attempt to pre-empt and prevent the manifest reign of Christ on earth was short-lived and doomed to failure, because the fate of their master, the devil, was sealed on the cross (19:13; Col. 2:15). He is bound for a thousand years, during which time those martyred during the time of the beast reign with Christ. After this era, Satan makes one last attempt to regain control of the earth (referred to as the Gog and Magog battle which is described in Ezekiel 38 and 39). All antichrist forces are supernaturally defeated: 'And the devil, who deceived them, was thrown into the lake of burning sulphur, where the beast and the false prophet had been thrown. They will be tormented day and night for ever and ever' (Rev. 20:10).

Old earth – new earth

The final rebellion seals the fate, not only of the devil and his minions, but also of the earth. On his return to earth, Jesus gave the last chance to its inhabitants to acknowledge his lordship, without the malevolent influence of Satan to weaken their resolve to do so. The reader is told little about the Millennium, except that, despite all its glories, rebellion against God which is so ingrained in the human condition surfaces in the end. That is the reason why God's ultimate judgment for the earth has to take place: 'Earth and sky fled from [God's] presence, and there was no place for them' (20:11). The Last Judgment of human beings is also described (20:11–15), leading to 'the second death' for all whose names are not written in the 'book of life'. Death and hell are also 'thrown into the lake of fire', giving credence to the view of those who believe in annihilation, at some point, for those outside of Christ.

It is now possible for the new heaven and earth to come into view, their splendours almost beyond description. The glorious consummation of God's purpose for humanity is accomplished: 'Now the dwelling of God is with men, and he will live with them. They will be his people, and God himself will be with them and be their God.' An expression of poignant tenderness follows: 'He will wipe every tear from their eyes.' Suddenly all the horrendous judgments are seen in perspective. God himself had never caused death, mourning, crying or pain. These things belonged to the old order (21:4), having been brought about by demonic activity and human sin. Such rebellion against God had to be judged and removed, because of its legacy of untold human misery. It rendered necessary the death of his Son, and brought grief to the heart of God. In its place, the one on the throne declares: 'I am making everything new! . . . It is done. I am the Alpha and Omega, the Beginning and the End' (21:5–6). The kingdom of God and his Christ is at last fully revealed.

The perfect Church

There follows a description of the Church (the bride, the wife of the Lamb – 21:9), at the heart of the kingdom. The picture language used on this occasion is of a city with twelve foundations, decorated with precious stones, each layer with the name of one of the twelve apostles. The twelve gates are each made of a single pearl, inscribed with the names of the twelve tribes of Israel. The church of Jew and Gentile was always intended to be united, but only here does that unity reach perfection. The structure of this new Jerusalem – a huge cube – probably indicates that there is room for all believers. There is no temple, or source of light, because the Lord God and the Lamb are its temple and lamp. The river of life ceaselessly flows from the throne of God, continually nourishing all who drink from it with the life of God. The tree of life, first described in the book of Genesis, is found here at the end of the Bible, its leaves healing the nations, its abundant fruit available to all, for the curse of the Fall has been removed. Mention of nations reveals there is still a world to be ruled – the kingdom is always wider than the Church, even including the whole created order too. God's servants will see the face of the Lamb, and his name is on their foreheads (symbolically, in contrast with the name or number of human authority – 666 – mentioned in chapter 13). They will not be idle, but rather will reign for ever and ever, in positions of varying authority in the kingdom.

Final reminders

After all these dramatic visions, John is reminded that: 'The Lord, the God of the spirits of the prophets, sent his angel to show his servants the things that must soon take place' (22:6). In the last sixteen verses of the book of Revelation there are no fewer than three reminders from Jesus himself, that he is coming soon (22:7, 12, 20). The book, and indeed the whole Bible, concludes with reminders of the nature and character of Jesus; warnings not to detract from this prophecy; and an offer from the Spirit and the Church of the free gift of the water of life to all who are thirsty for God, who respond to the appeal to '*Come!*' Those who respond listen to the insistent reminders that Jesus will *come*, and utter no other response than: 'Amen. *Come*, Lord Jesus.'

Chapter **9**

Can the Last Things be summarised?

'He will come again in glory to judge the living and the dead, and his kingdom will have no end.'

(The Nicene Creed,
The Alternative Service Book 1980)

Putting it simply

If we had attempted to give even more basic answers than we already have in this book, when considering huge issues connected with the End Times, including the Second Coming and the Last Things (death, judgment, heaven and hell) it might well have been said that we had not understood the questions! A summary of what has been written so far, however, could be found useful, although it will inevitably be over-simplified. In this chapter we shall begin with a bird's-eye view of the relevant teaching in the New Testament, some of which has already been covered, but not yet in an ordered way. The summary of this book follows, after which we outline twelve points about eschatology, which issued from a consultation of church leaders with a deep interest in the subject, who represented different views but were able to reach considerable agreement.

A bird's-eye view of the Last Things in the New Testament

In this heading and the chapter heading we are using the phrase 'the Last Things' to include 'the End Times', as well. Although much of the New Testament teaching on the topics relevant to this book has been touched on already, it is important to see an overview, to gain a sense of perspective. If this is tackled according to the order of the books in the New Testament, just as we attempted to do briefly with respect to the Old Testament (apart from the minor prophets), it will help those who want to do further biblical study on eschatology. Even though we shall highlight teaching specific to the Last Things and the End Times, in one sense the entire New Testament is about the 'End', because Jesus is the End as well as the Beginning; he is the Last as well as the First; he is Omega as well as Alpha. The answer to all ultimate questions and the meaning of life itself are to be found in him. God's rescue plan for the human race was based on the life, death and resurrection of his Son, and the eternal life which he offers is actually the life of Jesus, who said: 'I am the way and the truth and the life. No-one comes to the Father except through me' (John 14:6). Since true life is only to be found in Jesus, the source of life, only those whose lives are bound up in his, through trust and love, actually have eternal life (which begins now and lasts for ever). Through his death and resurrection, Jesus declared victory over sin, death and hell – but there is the 'now', and the 'not yet'. When an individual receives God's offer of salvation now, the Holy Spirit gives a foretaste and a guaranteed promise of what is to come, when Satan is defeated and God's dwelling is with his people in heaven on earth.

In **Matthew, Mark and Luke** (the synoptic gospels), it is clear right away that the main emphasis in the teaching of Jesus was that he had come to announce *the kingdom* or rule of God. This message fails to impact the contemporary reader as much as it did the Jews. They had been longing for this prophetic message for centuries – but it required a change of mind-set to realise that this special kingdom was to be totally different from any earthly empire, and was to be inaugurated (after initial signs of healing and exorcisms, etc.) by the death and resurrection of the longed-for Messiah, the account of which takes up one-third of the gospels. Today, much of the world has outgrown the idea of kingdoms ruled by a sovereign. Democracy is regarded as the ideal, emphasising the rights and freedom of individuals. Any concept of submission to a supreme ruler tends to generate a response of antagonism and rebellion. That is why it is vital to note the balance in the teaching of Christ, including that on God as the perfect Father, who delights to respond to the prayers of his children. Jesus also showed by deed as well as word, that: 'The Spirit of the Lord is on me, because he has anointed me to preach good news to the poor. He has sent me to proclaim freedom for the prisoners and recovery of sight for the blind, to release the oppressed, to proclaim the year of the Lord's favour' (Luke 4:18–19). In teaching such as the Sermon on the Mount, Jesus showed that the values of the kingdom of heaven are the opposite of worldly values. Only in his service is true freedom to be found – to deny self for Christ is the way to discover life.

The *prophetic teaching* of Jesus about the signs of the times and his return has already been covered in this book (Chapter 4). It is to be found mostly in Matthew 24 and 25, Mark 13 and Luke 17 and 21. In Matthew 25 three interesting parables are recorded: the story of the wise and foolish bridesmaids emphasises the need to be alert, for no one knows the time of the arrival of the bridegroom (Jesus); whereas the parable of the talents shows the importance of making the most of our time on this earth, to use the gifts God has given us in his service. The parable of the sheep and the goats stresses how essential it is that such service includes caring for the poor, the needy, the oppressed, the sick and people whom we would regard as 'strangers'. As the nations are arrayed before Christ at the Last Judgment, these are the main criteria by which he judges the people. Failure to fulfil those obligations will result in eternal punishment.

The Gospel of John emphasises rather different aspects of Jesus' teaching. The following verses sum up many of its dominant themes related to eschatology:

For God so loved the world that he gave his one and only Son, that whoever believes in him shall not perish but have eternal life. For God did not send his Son into the world to condemn the world, but to save the world through him . . . This is the verdict: Light has come into the world, but men loved darkness instead of light because their deeds were evil . . . But whoever lives by the truth comes into the light, so that it may be seen plainly that what he has done has been done through God. (John 3:16–21)

The Acts of the Apostles begins with the story of the birth of the Church, when the Holy Spirit filled the disciples with power to extend the kingdom of God. It is interesting that Jesus in his recorded teaching emphasised the kingdom but only mentioned the Church twice, whereas the book of Acts and the epistles are packed with teaching on the Church. Theologians have debated ever since the relationship between the two concepts. Here there is only space to point out that the kingdom is far wider than the Church – God intends to reveal his sovereignty throughout the world one day, fulfilling all that Jesus inaugurated. The Church, the corporate body of his followers, was to be his instrument to exemplify and extend the kingdom. In his first sermon, Peter referred to the Second Coming of Jesus, and quoted a prophecy from the book of Joel which has an end-time reference, even though there is a sense in which the Last Days began when the Holy Spirit came at Pentecost. It is clear from the first that the age of the Church continues until the Lord of the Church returns.

The Epistle to the Romans contains, as we have stressed in Chapter 7 of this book, major teaching on the future of the Jewish people in chapters 9–11. In addition to many other vital themes, including justification by grace through faith, which leads to peace with God now and in eternity, there is thrilling teaching on a glorious future for creation, when the children of God are 'revealed':

I consider that our present sufferings are not worth comparing with the glory that will be revealed in us. The creation waits in eager expectation for the sons of God to be revealed. For the creation was subjected to frustration, not by its own choice, but by the will of the one who subjected it, in hope that the creation itself will be liberated from its bondage to decay and brought into the glorious freedom of the children of God. We know that the whole creation has been groaning as in the pains of childbirth right up to the present time. Not only so, but we ourselves, who have the firstfruits of the Spirit, groan inwardly as we wait eagerly for our adoption as sons, the redemption of our bodies. (Rom. 8:18–23)

This passage makes clear that there is something awry throughout the created order, which will only be remedied when the body is redeemed (a reference to the resurrection of the body and the creation of the new heaven and earth).

In **the Corinthian Epistles**, there is quite lengthy teaching on the resurrection of Christ and Christians, which is stressed as being absolutely essential to the gospel (1 Cor. 15). Earlier, St Paul had taught that what believers build on the foundation of their faith in Christ will be scrutinised on Judgment Day (3:10–15), and the saints will judge the world and angels (6:2, 3). Of great importance is the teaching on the Lord's Supper, where one major emphasis is: 'For whenever you eat this bread and drink this cup, you proclaim the Lord's death *until he comes*' (11:26). In 2 Corinthians 4 and 5, wonderful truths are conveyed about the surpassing glory which awaits those who are in Christ. Even in the present age: 'the light of the knowledge of the glory of God in the face of Christ' (4:6) shines in our hearts, but is partially hidden in 'jars of clay' (4:7) – a reference to the physical body, vulnerable to numerous afflictions prior to the resurrection.

In **the Epistle to the Galatians**, the following important principle is taught:

Do not be deceived: God cannot be mocked. A man reaps what he sows. The one who sows to please his sinful nature, from that nature will reap destruction; the one who sows to please the Spirit, from the Spirit will reap eternal life. Let us not become weary in doing good, for at the proper time we will reap a harvest if we do not give up. Therefore, as we have opportunity, let us do good to all people, especially to those who belong to the family of believers. (Gal. 6:7–10)

This underlines that God's judgment is to allow people to reap the consequences of their thoughts, words and deeds in this life and the next.

The Epistle to the Ephesians is almost entirely about God's overall purposes for his people, which makes it one of the most significant books in the Bible in connection with the subject of the Last Things, even though it does not include any teaching in detail on such matters as judgment, heaven and hell, or the Second Coming. The whole of chapter 1 is devoted to an overview of God's plans for the Church and the world, which we shall look at in more detail in our last chapter. Chapter 2 is about salvation and reconciliation; in chapter 3 St Paul beautifully describes in even greater depth God's ultimate purpose for the Church. In the second half of chapter 6 the reader is given clear insight into the battle in heavenly realms between forces of light and darkness, good and evil, God and the devil, which forms the backdrop to the struggles of believers in this life, and makes it imperative to put on God-given armour (of faith, salvation, righteousness, the word of God, prayer, etc.) to be able to stand firm.

In **the Epistle to the Philippians** we note two key references for our present purpose: 'God exalted him to the highest place and gave him the name that is above every name, that at the name of Jesus every knee should bow, in heaven and on earth and under the earth, and every tongue confess that Jesus Christ is Lord, to the glory of God the Father' (Phil. 2:9–11). Later, Paul writes: 'But our citizenship is in heaven. And we eagerly await a Saviour from there, the Lord Jesus Christ, who, by the power that enables him to bring everything under his control, will transform our lowly bodies so that they will be like his glorious body' (Phil. 3:20–1).

The Epistle to the Colossians is comparable to Ephesians, in expressing the depth of the insights given by the Holy Spirit to St Paul about the wonder of God's wider purposes. Extracts from chapter 1 have been quoted on a number of occasions in this book – for example, that: 'God was pleased to have all his fulness dwell in him, and through him to reconcile to himself all things, whether things on earth or things in heaven, by making peace through his blood, shed on the cross' (Col. 1:19–20). Eschatology is all about God's plans in and through Jesus: to bring to completion everything in union with Christ.

In **1 and 2 Thessalonians** explicit teaching is given about the Second Coming. We have already described much of the teaching in chapter 4 about the return of Christ and the resurrection of the dead. The contrast with the first two chapters of 2 Thessalonians could not be more marked. This is a clear example of dual-aspect prophecy – where the same future event is described from two such totally different perspectives that some have mistakenly concluded that there must be two returns of Christ! Rather, the beautiful description in the first epistle is about the wonder of the dramatic return of Jesus for those whose lives have already been transformed by his power. But in the second epistle we read:

> This will happen when the Lord Jesus is revealed from heaven in blazing fire with his powerful angels. He will punish those who do not know God and do not obey the gospel of our Lord Jesus. They will be punished with everlasting destruction and shut out from the presence of the Lord and from the majesty of his power on the day he comes to be glorified in his holy people and to be marvelled at among all those who have believed. (2 Thess. 1:7–10)

Three words are used in the Greek to describe the Second Coming of Christ: one is *epiphaneia* ('appearing'), drawing attention to the visibility of his return (1:7); the second is *parousia*, meaning 'arrival', as in the visit of a ruler (2:1); and the third is *apokalypsis*, meaning an 'unveiling' of his power and glory (2:8).

There are also fascinating details in chapter 2 about *'the man of lawlessness'* which we have not yet touched on, but which may be linked, as we shall see, with certain teaching in Revelation (some of the biblical writers were familiar with each other's epistles). St Paul stresses that Jesus will not return until 'the rebellion occurs and the man of lawlessness is revealed, the man doomed to destruction. He will oppose and will exalt himself over everything that is called God or is worshipped, so that he sets himself up in God's temple, proclaiming himself to be God' (2:3–4). This could also be identified with 'the abomination that causes desolation' mentioned in Jesus' well-known prophecy, quoting from Daniel (Matt. 24:15; Dan. 9:27; 11:31; 12:11). As we have noted previously, there have been historical fulfilments, whether the word 'temple' is interpreted literally or as a metaphor of the Church as an organisation. *But what follows makes it clear that there will be an ultimate fulfilment immediately before the Second Coming, because 'the lawless one will be revealed, whom the Lord Jesus will overthrow with the breath of his mouth and destroy by the splendour of his coming'* (2:8). It is difficult to avoid the conclusion that the lawless one is the same as the beast in Revelation, who demands world-wide allegiance and adulation – ultimately even worship. Mention is made of counterfeit miraculous signs, which originate from Satan, deceiving 'those who are perishing. They perish because they refuse to love the truth and so be saved' (v. 10). This is in contrast to those who stand firm, believing the gospel, who are being sanctified by the Spirit, having been chosen by God to share the glory of Jesus (vv. 13–15).

There are two further intriguing points to note in chapter 2. One is that there appears to be 'someone' who is at present restraining the secret power of lawlessness which is already at work. The lawless one will only be revealed when this restraint is removed. This could refer to an angel, or to the Holy Spirit working through the visible Church – which, as we saw from Revelation chapters 12 and 13, may disappear 'underground' in the last persecution, thus removing from organised society a powerful influence in restraining evil. The second reference is to a powerful delusion sent (permitted) by God, leading to people believing 'the lie' – that the man of lawlessness is god. In fact, the first lie ever whispered by Satan into the ear of human beings was 'you will be like God, knowing good and evil' (Gen. 3:4). Ever since then, that desire has been at the heart of rebellion against God and his will. The powerful delusion could be unusual susceptibility to deceit, once any restraining influence for good has been removed. We know that something of that scenario was the case in Nazi Germany and Maoist China, to name but two instances. It would be foolish to deny that it could happen swiftly on an international scale, particularly in an age of global communications. Besides, in our times, we have witnessed the amazing phenomenon of world-wide mourning for Princess Diana sweeping nations in a few days, and apparently somewhere between a quarter and a third of the world population watching or listening to the broadcast of her funeral service. Although that emotion of grief was obviously not evil, it demonstrates how quickly the world could be affected by a powerful movement, emotion, attitude or viewpoint, whether good or evil.

That leaves unanswered a puzzling question, which we have not yet addressed. If there is to be a terrible demonic deceit affecting the whole world, albeit briefly, just before the return of Jesus, how is it that his return could still be unexpected – wouldn't it be obvious that the time is near? Why are Christians warned to be alert, because Jesus could return at any time, if prophecies such as these in 2 Thessalonians remain to be fulfilled? The only answer can be that there is a fluidity about end-time prophecy (allowing several provisional fulfilments), and a certain mystery, so that no one should think that every detail can be tied up – rather, the reality will far transcend expectations. Much is deliberately left unexplained by the Holy Spirit, so that the Church should always be alert.

In the pastoral epistles (**1 and 2 Timothy** and **Titus**) there are more general references to terrible times in the Last Days, when people will be lovers of themselves, rather than of God, having a form of godliness but denying its power. The time will come when people will not put up with sound doctrine. But if we endure, we shall also reign with Jesus, and there is a crown of righteousness in store for all who have longed for his appearing, fighting the good fight of faith. It will be awarded by the Lord, the righteous Judge (1 Tim. 6:14; 2 Tim. 2:12; 3:1–5; 4:1–8). The arrival 'of our great God and Saviour, Jesus Christ' will be glorious (Titus 2:13).

The brief personal letters to **Philemon** and Gaius (**3 John**) are the only books in the New Testament without any references to eschatology.

In **the Epistle to the Hebrews,** we read at the beginning of the book that the heavens will perish, but the Lord remains; and at the end, that God will once more shake the earth and the heavens, indicating the removal of created things, so that the kingdom which cannot be shaken will remain (Heb. 1:11; 12:26–9). Everything will be subject to Jesus, who is crowned with glory and honour and will bring many sons to glory. Meanwhile he waits for his enemies to become his footstool. He will destroy the devil and free those who were held in slavery by fear of death. For those who keep on sinning there is only a fearful expectation of judgment, but true believers should encourage one another as they see the Day approaching. In fact, Jesus who is coming will come and will not delay. Man is destined once to die, then to face judgment. God is a consuming fire (Heb. 2:5–15; 9:27–8; 10:13, 25–7, 35–9).

James admonishes his readers in his epistle to 'be patient and stand firm, because the Lord's coming is near . . . The Judge is standing at the door!' (5:8–9). Those who persevere under trial 'will receive the crown of life that God has promised to those who love him' (1:12).

In **the Epistles of Peter** there is considerable teaching on the Last Things. From the first letter we learn that the new birth brings wonderful hope of a heavenly inheritance. This is for those who are shielded by God's power through faith, until the (fulness of) salvation comes that is ready to be revealed in the last time (1 Pet. 1:3–9). The writer stresses that the end of all things is near. The living and the dead will be judged, but judgment begins with the family of God. This being the case, 'if it is hard for the righteous to be saved, what will become of the ungodly and the sinner?' (4:7, 17–19) There is a special promise for overseers in the Church – as 'shepherds of God's flock', when 'the Chief Shepherd appears, you will receive the crown of glory that will never fade away' (5:1–4).

In his second letter, Peter uses a beautiful phrase to describe the moment in the next life when the believer meets Jesus: 'the day dawns and the morning star rises in your hearts' (1:19). By contrast, the ungodly will be held by the Lord for the Day of Judgment, 'while continuing their punishment' (2:9), and rebellious angels are kept in 'gloomy dungeons' awaiting judgment (2:4). Peter anticipates that in the last days, scoffers will mockingly ask: 'Where is this "coming" he promised?' His answer is: 'With the Lord a day is like a thousand years, and a thousand years are like a day. The Lord is not slow in keeping his promise, as some understand slowness. He is patient with you, not wanting anyone to perish, but everyone to come to repentance' (3:8–9). Teaching is given, in the same chapter, about the present heaven and earth being reserved for the Day of Judgment and destruction of the ungodly; the heavens will disappear with a roar, and the earth will be laid bare, when the Day of the Lord comes 'like a thief'. Here there seems to be no time-lapse of an earthly millennium between the Second Coming and the new heaven and earth – but one needs to remember the concertina effect, as Peter looked ahead prophetically.

In the first two **Epistles of John**, a new term is introduced: 'the antichrist'. St John writes: 'Dear children, this is the last hour; and as you have heard that the antichrist is coming, even now many antichrists have come. This is how we know it is the last hour . . . Who is the liar? It is the man who denies that Jesus is the Christ. Such a man is the antichrist – he denies the Father and the Son' (1 John 2:18, 22). In 1 John 4:3 we read: 'but every spirit that does not acknowledge Jesus is not from God. This is the spirit of the antichrist, which you have heard is coming and even now is already in the world.' In the second epistle, verse 7, John re-emphasises: 'Many deceivers, who do not acknowledge Jesus Christ as coming in the flesh, have gone out into the world. Any such person is the deceiver and the antichrist.' The Greek word *anti* means 'in place of', which obviously can be developed to mean 'in opposition to'. John was warning believers about an early form of the heresy which became known as Gnosticism, in which salvation was thought to be gained through knowledge of certain secrets, known only to the initiated. This included denial of Jesus' humanity. John had discerned that there was a particular demonic spirit, the spirit of antichrist, behind this deception and behind any other attempt to replace the true Jesus of revelation with a Jesus of imagination. *John's teaching is that there is one antichrist spirit, with many human manifestations.*

It is possible that John's letters were written after the book of Revelation, which means that, even if the author is not the same John (the style of the epistles and gospel are very similar, but that of Revelation is very different), it is probable that he knew the teaching about the beast, and, of course, Jesus' teaching, quoting Daniel, of the abomination of desolation (possibly an image to be worshipped, installed by a powerful figure). He would also have known St Paul's terminology about the man of lawlessness. It is highly likely that all these references are different ways of viewing a terrible blasphemy, which will have an ultimate fulfilment in the End Times, but many interim manifestations in place of and/or opposed to Christ. Many examples of this may be seen in history, including the christ advocated by Jehovah's Witnesses (who deny the Trinity), or the christ spirit spoken of by some New Agers, which is said to indwell a number of prophetic figures, including Jesus. It tends to be unfashionable in theological circles to believe in an ultimate embodiment of the antichrist spirit, because that is seen as an over-literal end-time scenario. But it seems clear that the early Christians, who knew the prophecies of Jesus, Paul and John, would have expected not only a literal return of Jesus, but leading up to that a final manifestation of the antichrist spirit, which would be overthrown by the victorious Christ. Since the vast majority of the Christian Church world-wide still hold strongly to the former, it is our contention that there is no good reason to disbelieve the latter. In fact, a final demonic rebellion of some kind is almost inevitable. But John reminds believers in every age: 'You, dear children, are from God and have overcome them, because the one who is in you is greater than the one who is in the world' (1 John 4:4).

From the short **Epistle of Jude**, it is only necessary to quote a couple of references: 'See, the Lord is coming with thousands upon thousands of his holy ones to judge everyone, and to convict all the ungodly of all the ungodly acts they have done in the ungodly way, and of all the harsh words ungodly sinners have spoken against him' (Jude 14–15). 'But you, dear friends, build yourselves up in your most holy faith and pray in the Holy Spirit.

Keep yourselves in God's love as you wait for the mercy of our Lord Jesus Christ to bring you to eternal life' (Jude 20–1).

The book of Revelation has already been summarised in depth, in our previous chapter.

The overview above reveals an amazing unity and complementarity of vision throughout the New Testament, and may itself be summarised in a rather simplistic way:

A simplified summary of teaching on the Last Things (Matthew – Jude)

- People are destined to die once, after which they face judgment
- They reap what they sow, leading to eternal life, or eternal punishment
- The criterion for salvation is belief in the Son of God
- A great gulf is fixed at death
- The ungodly, and sinful angels, are held for judgment
- Believers are with Christ when they die
- Jesus will come in the same manner in which he ascended
- The Second Coming is preceded by signs
- It will be sudden, dramatic and seen world-wide
- Jesus will be accompanied by those who have died trusting in him
- Their bodies will be resurrected and transformed, as will the bodies of believers who are alive at the time
- Unbelievers are left
- The nations mourn
- There is sudden destruction
- Believers will reign with Christ and judge Israel/nations/angels
- Final judgment begins with the family of God, who are saved by faith but judged according to what they have built on the foundation of Christ
- The Son is the Judge – everyone will bow before him
- Those who inherit eternal life are immortal
- The present heavens and earth are reserved for the destruction of the ungodly

- The devil and death will be destroyed
- There will be a new heaven and earth
- God's kingdom will come on earth as in heaven
- The incomparable riches of God's grace will be revealed to believers
- Everything will be united under Christ

The story so far

What follows is the summary of Chapters 1–8 of this book:

In **Chapter 1** (*'What on earth will happen?'*), we began with the bad news about what the Bible has to say about the future of planet Earth. We showed that the dire warnings and catastrophic visions presented in the Scriptures can no longer be dismissed by the world as religious lunacy: we are becoming ever more aware of the man-made and natural possibilities of destruction (earthly and cosmic) which our planet faces. We turned to even more central reasons for taking the Bible seriously, whether about the beginning or the end of the world, even though it is not a scientific text-book. By 'world', we were reminded that the Scriptures are about God's purposes for the earth and its inhabitants. There are very few references to the future of the whole universe. What they do make clear is that God is the Creator of all its vast array, and not only was his Son the agent of creation, but it was all for him in the first place. Tragically, it seems that evil came on the scene when the mighty angel, later known as Satan, rebelled against God. He appears to have been allowed a certain amount of power over the earth and *may* have introduced disorder, but this would not have caused death (in the normal sense of the term) to human beings had they not fallen to temptation. The consequences of sin were and are utterly devastating, but God had already planned redemption through his Son. The Bible is the story of the still unfolding plan of salvation, and therefore is intrinsically prophetic. Everything will one day be reconciled in Christ (Col. 1:15–20), but before that happens there will be terrible destruction, including of the earth, whether in part or in whole.

In **Chapter 2** ('*Is there life after life?*'), we shared the good news of the New World Order which God has planned when he creates the new earth – in fact, heaven will be on earth, in the sense that God will dwell with his people. Most theologians believe in the re-creation of the old earth, but other views were mentioned too. Life in heaven on earth will be no spooky existence, but rather the fulfilment of all that God the Father has planned for his children. They will see his Son face to face, experience true joy eternally, untarnished by suffering of any kind, and will be engaged in co-operating with God's purposes. What we know of Jesus resurrected from the dead is a foretaste of what God has in store for believers: an existence which transcends all expectations and limitations in this life. Having considered heaven on earth as it will be after the destruction of the present order, we thought about where heaven (the present abode of the angels of God) might be now. The possibility was suggested that it is all around us in a largely unseen dimension, which on occasions breaks through into present awareness. Those who have died trusting in Christ may be in that dimension now, in spirit form (prior to the resurrection of the body), enjoying being with the angels, worshipping God in heaven. Another possibility is that they may be outside of time, or unaware of its passage, secure as they are in Christ. That could mean that the next event after death of which they are aware is returning with Christ to earth (1 Thess. 4:14), to be clothed in risen bodies. God will use his heavenly blueprint for each person in re-creation. Meanwhile, for those who are alive, trusting in Christ, heaven begins in the here and now, because at its heart is a relationship with God through Jesus. Sadly, death comes to all, but its sting was removed for believers by the resurrection of Christ, which signalled the destruction of the power of sin, death and hell.

In **Chapter 3** ('*Is hell out of date?*'), we considered that since justice is an aspect of the loving nature of God, judgment is inevitable. Jesus himself bore the judgment of God for sinners (all humanity), but justification, although offered to all, is only granted to those who repent and believe. Those who do not must be judged in the next life. Christ himself is the judge, and even believers must stand before him one day. Since they are 'in Christ', they already have eternal life, but a process of purification is necessary for remaining unconfessed deeds, words, thoughts and motives. There will be rewards according to one's character, life, and service – possibly differences in roles in heaven. Those who have ignored or rejected God's way of salvation are outside of Christ, the source of life, and are therefore denied eternal life. Sentences differ for each person according to way of life. It is unlikely that there is physical torment in hell, but some regard it as a place of everlasting regret and mental anguish. Others prefer to interpret references to the second death (Rev. 20:14) as meaning annihilation, after the Last Judgment. We put forward the idea of a temporal hell on the earth after the Last Judgment, but prior to the destruction of the planet and final annihilation of those human beings who have ignored or rejected the God of revelation. It is likely that those who have never had a realistic chance to hear and respond to the gospel will be treated as those who lived before Christ came, according to their response of faith in the revelation they have received from the Holy Spirit, especially of the one true Creator God. But salvation is only accomplished through Christ, the effects of whose death reach back in time as well as forward to the future.

In **Chapter 4** ('*Will Jesus ever return?*'), we looked at the contrast between the description in the Bible of the first coming of Jesus, and its portrayal of his return. Since so few of the Jewish scholars of the time recognised that Jesus was the Messiah, we were reminded that this should be taken as a salutary warning. It is possible to be so dogmatic about the interpretation of prophecies that one could be blind when their fulfilment transcends all expectations. Although the Second Coming itself is portrayed as a dramatic event which brings about the end of this present order, the signs leading up to it should be interpreted with caution. Having considered characteristics of biblical prophecy, we applied those to 'the signs of the times'. It became clear that there has been considerable fulfilment in various events throughout the last two thousand years; they also illuminate the on-going conflict between good and evil; but the twin signs of both world-wide evangelism and persecution seem to be indications that the return of Christ is at hand.

In **Chapter 5** ('*Will there be another millennium?*'), we described the different views about the biblical Millennium, reviewing their strengths and weaknesses, and recommending an attitude of mutual respect. We also suggested a 'pan-millennial' view which would encompass aspects of the three main views. While recognising that scenarios of the End Times would be simplified if there is no millennial reign of Christ after his return, but rather an immediate transition from the present order to the Last Judgment, we suggested a significant reason for such a Millennium. In particular, it would be a demonstration of Christ's sovereignty over the existing world order, over the nations, and indeed over creation as we know it.

In **Chapter 6** ('*Does the Old Testament shed light on the future?*'), we examined further the nature of biblical prophecy, before tracing teaching about the future from Genesis to Daniel. We stressed that although particular texts obviously need to be considered on their own merits and in their context, it is even more important to see the overview of God's purposes being revealed prophetically throughout Scripture, in particular his plan of salvation through his Son.

In **Chapter 7** ('*Does modern Israel figure in God's future purposes?*'), after describing briefly both sides of the Israeli–Palestinian conflict, we saw that Christians are divided over whether there is any prophetic significance in the land and contemporary nation of Israel. Nearly all, however, see it as God's merciful provision after the Holocaust. Most biblical comment-ators affirm from Romans 9–11 that God has a future purpose for the Jewish people: 'all Israel will be saved' (Rom. 11:26). Comparing this with other scriptures, it would appear that 'all Israel' refers to a significant minority of Jews (a third is mentioned in Zechariah 13:7–9). Their salvation will bring 'riches' to the rest of the world (Rom. 11:12), the nature of which is not specified, although a clearer understanding may be gained from Old Testament passages. We looked at some of those, concluding that a return of the Jews to the land of Israel in the Last Days was foretold long ago, together with prophecies that this would lead to international conflict and widespread repentance by the

Jewish people in connection with the Messiah, which would herald his return. We suggested that relevant Old Testament scriptures appear to show that God's purpose in restoring Jewish people to Israel (bearing in mind that his commands to treat other people-groups with justice apply as much as ever they did) is connected with the revelation of the lordship of Jesus over the nations in the millennium. This would lead to a period of blessing for the world.

In **Chapter 8** ('*Can Revelation be revealed?*'), we recommended a comprehensivist view, affirming that many of the prophecies had an initial historical fulfilment; that other fulfilments can be traced throughout history; that they throw light on the on-going conflict between good and evil; and that an ultimate fulfilment is likely. A major emphasis is that those suffering for their faith are given strong encouragement to persevere. St John's vantage point in heaven, glimpsing something of its glorious worship, renders his view of events on earth as all the more horrendous by contrast. The opening of the seal judgments reveals Jesus to be Lord even in traumatic circumstances. Most of the horrors described are caused by the sin of humanity, exacerbated by demonic activity. Even many natural disasters can be linked to the sin or mistakes of human beings. The multi-ethnic Church and Jewish people who become believers in the End Times are seen to be united in God's purposes in the Last Days. One futurist interpretation of prophecies in the second half of the book is that the glorious Church, being prepared to be presented as the bride of Christ, briefly disappears from view as an organisation (only to be revealed later as victorious) in the final world-wide persecution. Some believe this persecution will take place when the enemy attempts a counterfeit New World Order, to pre-empt and prevent the revelation of the kingdom of God. This demonic system is itself used as an instrument to judge the politico-economic systems (Babylon) on which the world has come to rely, but which embody so much that is opposed to the will of God. Jesus triumphs over the counterfeit kingdom at his Second Coming, revealing his sovereignty over the earth as we know it. Final rebellion leads to final defeat of the devil. The Last

Judgment takes place, prior to the revelation of the new heaven and earth. The dwelling of God will at last be with his people.

Unity on key issues

It will encourage readers to learn that, when the authors convened a consultation on eschatology in 1994 of a dozen church leaders of different denominations (one or two with higher academic qualifications in the subject), with different perspectives on the End Times (e.g. some held a classic pre-millennial position; some were post-millennialists, and some a-millennialists), all were able to agree on the following twelve points, which are stated in simplified form:

1 Since God always has the end in view, all true theology involves eschatology.
2 The return of Christ will be visible, bodily and glorious.
3 The resurrection of the body and the ultimate enjoyment by believers of the new heavens and earth which God will create.
4 The present transformation of believers through salvation and sanctification should be seen as the first instalment of their ultimate glorification.
5 There will be a Last Judgment.
6 Prophecy rarely exhausts its meaning in historical fulfilment, and events in history often foreshadow events near the End.
7 The Christian hope of the New Testament – that Jesus will return to complete the kingdom inaugurated at his first coming – is firmly rooted in, and grew out of, the hope of Israel.
8 All delegates affirmed emphases in the three main millennial views:
  • in pre-millennialism, awareness of intensification of evil before the End;
  • in a-millennialism, conviction that Christ is reigning now;
  • in post-millennialism, vision for world evangelisation.
9 The statement was welcomed of a delegate holding a **post-millennial** position that: 'Since . . . Paul forewarned of "terrible seasons" throughout the "last days" [which began

at Pentecost], the *a-millennialist* concept of *recurring* manifestations of the satanic kingdom . . . is . . . a helpful antidote against Western triumphalism . . . Indeed, the final "short time" could even see a world-wide re-enactment of the horrendous scenario of Revelation chapters 6–18, as the *pre-millennialists* teach.'

10 Eschatology is an important stimulus to sanctification and service, and Christians who hold to any of the millennial views can and do share an emphasis on evangelism.

11 It is important for Christians to pray for the return of Christ.

12 It is vital to convey these truths to fellow Christians.

It was also recognised that there was unlikely to be agreement, even between Christians with a similar view of Scripture, on the following points:

• The place of Israel in God's purposes
• How much has been fulfilled of relevant prophecies
• The correlation between the prophecies of Daniel and the future
• Whether there is a *secret* rapture of believers, and whether there is a one-stage or two-stage return of Christ
• The position and purpose of the Millennium
• The nature of hell
• The interpretation of the book of Revelation

Since that consultation, we have had a passion to emphasise that it is possible to achieve basic unity, and proclaim with certainty many major aspects of eschatology, while agreeing to disagree with mutual respect over some of the issues and recognising that the reality of the End Times will transcend all expectations.

Chapter 10

Is being heavenly minded any earthly use?

'We are looking forward to a new heaven and a new earth, the home of righteousness. So then... make every effort to be found spotless, blameless and at peace with [God].'

(2 Pet. 3:13–14)

Heavenly minded

The most basic understanding of biblical teaching and prophecy about the Last Things and the End Times can revolutionise the Christian life. We hope that this book has opened the eyes of readers to see that eschatology is at the heart of the Bible. It is a tragedy that most Christian leaders in the West neglect key aspects of this teaching for fear of being thought extreme, or of getting trapped in a maze of different views. Those who do make the effort to teach these subjects usually major on the relevance to life today. Although this is vital, these subjects are also very important in and of themselves, pointing as they do to realities in eternity. We want to emphasise that it is essential to know what the Bible teaches about the kingdom, eternal life with God, hell, the destiny of the earth, Israel, the Second Coming, etc., so that we understand something of what God has planned for humanity and planet Earth. Our heavenly Father expects us to take some of the wrappings off the presents which he has so carefully chosen for his children, in expectation of the very special gifts which he will allow us to see on the great day. It is biblical to be heavenly minded! Only those who become obsessed with these subjects, to the detriment of practical Christian living here and now, lose effectiveness. But we are meant to get excited! Something of the breadth, length, depth, height and sheer thrill of God's purposes is conveyed in this prayer:

> I keep asking that the God of our Lord Jesus Christ, the glorious Father, may give you the Spirit of wisdom and revelation, so that you may know him better. I pray also that the eyes of your heart may be enlightened in order that you may know the hope to which he has called you, the riches of his glorious inheritance in the saints, and his incomparably great power for us who believe. That power is like the working of his mighty strength, which he exerted in Christ when he raised him from the dead and seated him at his right hand in the heavenly realms, far above all rule and authority, power and dominion, and every title that can be given, not only in the present age but also in the one to come. And God placed all things under his feet and appointed him to be head over everything for the church, which is his body, the fulness of him who fills everything in every way. (Eph. 1:17–23)

Earthly use

The 'earthly use' of such a heavenly vision, however, cannot be overestimated. We shall list and enlarge on some aspects of that after the quotations below. Without some understanding (which means heart-knowledge, which the Holy Spirit gives to all who ask in faith, whatever their intellectual ability) of these subjects, individual Christians, or many a local church, could nibble their way through life with their heads down, like so many sheep, without a sense of purpose or destination. Having grasped initially something of the wonder of salvation through Jesus, Christians need to look ahead, and look up! There is no greater antidote to prevent Christians being mundane. Above all, appreciation deepens of the sovereignty of Jesus, when it is understood that he is the Lord of history:

> He is the image of the invisible God, the firstborn over all creation. For by him all things were created: things in heaven and on earth, visible and invisible, whether thrones or powers or rulers or authorities; all things were created by him and for him. He is before all things, and in him all things hold together. And he is the head of the body, the church; he is the beginning and the firstborn from among the dead, so that in everything he might have the supremacy. For God was pleased to have all his fulness dwell in him, and through him to reconcile to himself all things, whether things on earth or things in heaven, by making peace through his blood, shed on the cross. (Col. 1:15–20)

Greater depth in worship and prayer

Such understanding will elicit a response of awe and wonder in worship, which is sadly lacking in many churches. It does not depend on the gifts of the musicians, important though their contribution is, because such worship is God-inspired. A service could be proceeding as normal, when, suddenly or gradually, the Holy Spirit causes the congregation to become aware of the awesome majesty of God. This can also happen in the prayer life of an individual believer, leading to being lost in wonder, love and praise. We have sensed the awesomeness of God in great cathedrals or in humble parish churches; when worshipping with our own congregation in church or in the context of a home fellowship group; when enjoying God's creation or observing his power to transform lives; in private prayer or surprised by God while engaged in study or a mundane task.

In addition, an overview of God's purposes should lead to greater breadth of vision in intercessory prayer, giving content to the phrase in the Lord's prayer about the coming of God's kingdom. One can learn to pray for God's will to be done here and now: in personal life; the local church; the denomination; the universal Church; the nation; and international affairs. Our prayer is that the Church will also take up the cry: 'Come Lord Jesus', in the belief that this will be used by God in his purposes to bring about the transition from this present state of affairs, with all its imperfections, injustices, inhumanity and ingrained rebellion against God, to the next – whether the Second Coming, leading to a millennium on earth prior to the new earth, or a greater manifestation of the rule of God here and now before the return of Christ, or his sudden return, followed by the Last Judgment and the new heaven and earth. Whatever our millennial views, in the end there is no room for dogmatism, because God will bring about only his purpose, not our ideas, however biblical we may *think* them to be. The prayer request 'Maranatha' ('Come, O Lord!': 1 Cor. 16:22) should be made with humility, yet fervency. We were once privileged to lead a meeting in Kerala, India, when the Holy Spirit suddenly revealed to the congregation of hundreds of Christian students the urgency of praying for Jesus to return. They stood up and with one accord began to call out 'Maranatha! Maranatha!' The cry grew ever louder, lasting for about ten minutes. If this prayer were to be prayed throughout the world, much would be achieved in the purposes of God. Some hold back, through fear that they might be hastening the unleashing of judgments on the earth or greater persecution, prior to Jesus' return. Others, frankly, are not eager for their Lord to come back, being comfortable with things as they are. Most of us are extremely nervous at the thought of our own deaths and transition to glory, let alone the monumental transition for humanity and the earth, from this age to the age to come. How vital that we learn to trust our heavenly Father more to work out his purpose in love, and that we also rely on our Lord Jesus, whom we love and serve, to judge with perfect justice. How essential that we become so concerned for that justice to be perfectly restored on earth that, although we work for it now, we pray for its completion then. Who knows – if the Maranatha prayer were to be taken up internationally, the Father might hasten the return of the Son, who wants to return for a Bride longing for his arrival. Perhaps he even delays until that prayer is voiced world-wide.

Renewed confidence in the inspiration of Scripture

The word 'inspired', when used in connection with the Bible, is thought by many theologians to raise far more problems than it solves. This is not the place to examine the various arguments, but simply to point out that a study of prophecy in the Bible, even the elementary overview in this book, should help to restore confidence that the Holy Spirit was not only operative in the entire complex process through which the various books of the Bible were written and compiled, but revealed amazing truths to the writers for forthtelling, and astonishing insights for foretelling. It is a miracle of great magnitude that, despite the number of different authors and sources, the long time-lapse between the writing of the first book and the last, and numerous other factors which would normally conspire against harmony, there is a remarkable unity of message in Scripture, even though diverse facets of truth are being highlighted. We have tried to make it abundantly clear that this message is of God's plan of salvation in Jesus, conceived before eternity and awaiting fruition at the end of this age. In addition, the number of prophecies which have been fulfilled, both great and small, provides huge encouragement to believe for the fulfilment of the remainder. Whereas we have tried to discourage an over-literalistic or fundamentalist view, yet we are just as concerned to resist treating prophecies as referring only to generalities, when it is quite clear that many have already been fulfilled, including those specifically fulfilled by Jesus, giving confidence to expect specific fulfilments in the future.

Deeper commitment to extending the kingdom

Greater appreciation of the nature of God's kingdom, and its various phases (including before Christ, after Christ, possibly a millennial kingdom, and the perfect kingdom on the new earth) provides incentive to devote one's life to spreading kingdom values. Discouragement fades in the knowledge that any attempt to achieve this, however imperfect, will be used by God, not only now but in the future, when perfection comes. Extending the kingdom is not an optional extra for Christians, but part and parcel of being a follower of Jesus. But each Christian has a unique role to play. All of us are meant to demonstrate attitudes such as those described in the Beatitudes (but remembering that we can only achieve this with the daily help of the Holy Spirit):

> Blessed are the poor in spirit, for theirs is the kingdom of heaven.
> Blessed are those who mourn, for they will be comforted.
> Blessed are the meek, for they will inherit the earth.
> Blessed are those who hunger and thirst for righteousness, for they will be filled.
> Blessed are the merciful, for they will be shown mercy.
> Blessed are the pure in heart, for they will see God.
> Blessed are the peacemakers, for they will be called sons of God.
> Blessed are those who are persecuted because of righteousness, for theirs is the kingdom of heaven. (Matt. 5:3–10)

We are called to model these attitudes and other characteristics such as the fruit of the Spirit (Gal. 5:22–3) in family life, at work and in leisure pursuits, as well as in social concern and evangelism. Parents and teachers who bring children up in God's ways are extending the kingdom. Men and women in business who uphold standards such as honesty, integrity, giving value for money, etc., are spreading kingdom values. People in the caring professions who really do care, who put the welfare of people in their care first, are demonstrating kingdom priorities. Those who are prepared to engage in vital voluntary work, or who campaign for issues of social justice, or who are untiring in bringing the needs of the two-thirds world to the attention of the richer third – all are bringing about a tiny part of the answer to the Lord's prayer which is mainly about extending God's kingdom. Taking action which benefits the eco-system is also a way of fulfilling God's will. While doing that, it is important to take any and every opportunity to spread the essential message that God is Creator. Before going further, readers could take this opportunity to reassess the part God is calling them to play in enlarging the kingdom where it begins – here and now.

Fresh urgency in evangelism

If we really believe that those without Christ are already in the kingdom of darkness and, if they continue to ignore or reject him, will spend their existence beyond the grave banished from the presence of God, it should be impossible to rest content, unless we are constantly reviewing ways to share the good news about Jesus with others. An even greater motive should be that we are overwhelmed by the love of God, and long for as many people as possible to share in all that he has prepared for his children, here and in eternity. But the devil devises all kinds of strategies to hinder evangelism – apathy, apprehension about raising the subject, a sense of inferiority about what to convey, guilt, discouragement, fear of creating barriers in relationships, and many more. We once ran an evangelism course which included practical opportunities to share the gospel with enquirers, only to find that nearly all the team members would feel physically unwell on that particular evening each week, or have a minor car accident, or be inordinately delayed in rush-hour traffic. Having recognised the enemy strategy, prayed against it and resolved to press on despite hindrances, we noticed that such incidents no longer seemed to be happening in that particular context.

The appropriate way to carry out evangelism will vary from culture to culture. In England at present, when endeavouring to share the gospel with adults in a typically middle-class environment, it is better to build bridges of genuine friendship, giving people opportunities over a period of time to take gradual steps of faith. Children are usually receptive in relevant fast-moving, multi-media events. In many parts of the world, big crusades are appropriate, while people in a situation of persecution may in some cases be reached by a Christian radio station or a portion of Scripture. Every Christian is called to be a witness to the Faith, but we all have different gifts. Some might be able to preach a powerful gospel sermon; others will have an obvious ministry to individuals, with the ability to take, or even create, opportunities. Some can lead an enquirers' group; some are gifted in youth work; others have a ministry of caring, which although important in and of itself, can also lead to opportunities to share one's faith. Some may be used by God to enthuse and mobilise a local church in creative methods of fulfilling an on-going programme of evangelism. It is very encouraging to the Christian who is there at the time of 'reaping', when an enquirer actually verbalises commitment to Christ for the first time. But there may have been a long chain of people who were used by God in the 'seed-sowing' process, some of whom never see the end result. Once again, readers could assess how their gifts are being, or could be, used in witnessing to their faith.

Greater encouragement to be overcomers

Many of the believers who were the recipients of the messages to the churches in the book of Revelation were either suffering for their faith or concerned that the dark clouds of persecution were looming. After a clear reminder of the Second Coming in the first chapter, the messages to them follow in chapters 2 and 3. Time and again Jesus commends them for patient endurance, or strongly urges them to stand firm, promising rewards in heaven for those who overcome:

> *To the church in Ephesus*: You have persevered and have endured hardships for my name, and have not grown weary (Rev. 2:3). To him who overcomes, I will give the right to eat from the tree of life (2:7). *To the church in Smyrna*: Do not be afraid of what you are about to suffer. I tell you, the devil will put some of you in prison to test you, and you will suffer persecution . . . Be faithful, even to the point of death, and I will give you the crown of life (2:10, 11). *To the church in Pergamum*: You did not renounce your faith in me, even in the days of Antipas, my faithful witness, who was put to death in your city (2:13). *To the church in Thyatira*: I know your deeds, your love and faith, your service and perseverance, and that you are now doing more than you did at first (2:19). To him who overcomes and does my will to the end, I will give authority over the nations . . . just as I have received authority from my Father (2:26–7). *To the church in Sardis*: Yet you have a few people in Sardis who have not soiled their clothes . . . He who overcomes will, like them, be dressed in white. I will never blot out his

name from the book of life, but will acknowledge his name before my Father and his angels (3:4–5). *To the church in Philadelphia*: Since you have kept my command to endure patiently, I will also keep you from the hour of trial that is going to come upon the whole world to test those who live on the earth. I am coming soon. Hold on to what you have, so that no one will take your crown. Him who overcomes I will make a pillar in the temple of my God . . . and I will also write on him my new name (3:10–12). *To the church in Laodicea*: To him who overcomes, I will give the right to sit with me on my throne, just as I overcame and sat down with my Father on his throne (3:21).

There can be no doubt that the promise of the glorious return of Jesus, and the wonders of heaven on earth to follow, helped to keep faith not just alive but triumphant, in those dark days of the early Church. This has been the case in other generations. Many Negro Spirituals, birthed in the ignominy of slavery, major on the theme of heaven. Belief in the Second Coming has, in recent persecutions, strengthened the faith of millions of Christians in China, who chose to belong to the 'underground' rather than officially permitted Church partly because, in the latter, teaching on the return of Christ is forbidden. Knowledge that Jesus will one day demonstrate his victory on the cross over all the powers of darkness enables believers to ask the Holy Spirit for strength to overcome in their time of trial now. Hope is such a vital concept in the Bible: it is not the vague wishful thinking of the world, but the sure and certain knowledge that God will fulfil his promises.

It may be that readers are not facing persecution, but opposition of a lesser kind to their faith, from family members or work colleagues. Perhaps different onslaughts to faith are being encountered: doubts, fears, temptations to apathy, laziness, immorality, self-indulgence, anger, hatred, materialism, envy and many other attacks. Many Christians would be ashamed if Jesus were to return today – their lives bear such a close resemblance to the lives of unbelievers that they are scarcely recognisable as the Bride of Christ. Rather than wallow in condemnation, we should ask forgiveness, claim God's power to be different, get in training for reigning: learn to serve our Lord now, so that he can use us in his eternal purposes then, in ways beyond imagination. Almost every reference to eschatology in the New Testament is followed by strong encouragement to live holy lives. Unfortunately the concept of holiness is not one which is immediately attractive, associated as it is with piety, which can seem dull and unappealing. But Jesus defined holiness (living according to God's will and laws) as love to God and neighbour, which he further defined as self-giving. Holiness immediately begins to sound much more attractive. Jesus said that those who live like that will inherit eternal life (Luke 10:25–37).

Better understanding of the place of the Church in God's purposes

It is impossible to have a proper understanding of much of the teaching of the Bible, unless it is recognised that God's purposes are corporate. The individual is important and, by contrast with the Communist ideal, is never a cog in a wheel or a means to an end. The overwhelming love of God for each person, however seemingly insignificant, prevents that from ever being the case. But one can only begin to grasp the sheer magnitude of God's plans if it is realised that God chose a people for himself: first the Jews, then the Church, where all barriers of race and gender are broken down. Sadly the Church has a tarnished reputation. It is clear from the New Testament that problems of various kinds arose even in the early years. After three centuries, it gradually became politicised as a powerful organisation, eventually controlling vast worldly resources, sometimes acting as an instrument of oppression. Heresies and divisions at times even gave rise to wars between rival factions. Praise God that true faith and holiness were never quenched, but burned brightly in various times of renewal, and even in times of darkness, in the lives of individuals, groups, monasteries and local manifestations of the Church. Much good was also still achieved through the Church as an organisation, even at the heights of power of the Catholic and Orthodox Churches, although the former reached its lowest point just before the Reformation. Today, denominations proliferate, but where once there was rivalry, in many cases there is greater co-operation at the time of the dawn of the third millennium than at any other since divisions multiplied. Even so, the image of the Church in the West is poor. Any evangelist knows that it is relatively easy to interest someone in the Faith, but far more difficult to encourage participation in the local church. Either there is disillusionment with its failings, or fears of curtailment of freedom by what is seen as life membership – or even life sentence! Some Christians become so discouraged by the petty attitudes prevalent in many churches that they only attend on Sunday, perhaps occasionally, refusing to be involved in the whole life of the local and wider church.

Painting such a black picture, of course, seriously misrepresents the enormous riches of life in the Church world-wide: the glorious diversity and profundity of worship, from the best cathedral service to the liveliest black gospel meeting; the unceasing wave of prayer from sunrise to sunset, whether expressed in adoration, confession, thanksgiving or intercession; the preaching, teaching, writing and studying of God's word; the fellowship enjoyed by Christians; the vast amount of sacrificial, often voluntary caring expressed in so many different ways; evangelism carried out in huge rallies, evangelistic services, small groups, person to person; work done among children; artistic achievements, whether great cathedrals, parish churches, paintings, sculptures, literature, music – the list is endless.

While bearing in mind this wealth of life and creativity, it is also important to step back and look at God's overall intentions for the Church, because an enlarged vision can help to play a part in the more local context. Jesus majored in his teaching on the kingdom; Paul majored on the Church. It had to be that way. No one would have understood if Jesus had taught about the Church prior to his crucifixion, resurrection, ascension and the outpouring of the Spirit. The disciples found it hard enough when Jesus taught a radical view of the kingdom. We now know that the rule of God is world-wide, and encompasses creation, nations, governments and the whole of humanity – not to mention the universe. The Church is a major aspect of that kingdom, composed of all those who acknowledge Jesus as Lord, at different stages of faith, from the tiniest flickering candle flame to a burning torch. But each is part of a bigger whole: the Body of Christ, of which Christ is the head. Together, whether in a localised manifestation of that Body, or seen from God's viewpoint as an international whole, stretching back and forwards in time, the Church is a vast dynamic living organism, highly significant in God's eyes.

Only the Church offers worship to God in the name of his Son; only the Church reaches out to others to involve them in that worship; only the Church encourages people to make the transition from the kingdom of darkness to the kingdom of light announced by Jesus; only the Church co-operates with God's purposes through intercession in the name of Jesus; only the Church cares for others overtly in that name, thus giving the glory to him. In his book *Theology and the Kingdom of GOD*, Wolfhart Pannenberg comments: 'The Church confronts the person with the ultimate fulfilment of life promised in the coming of God's future' (The Westminster Press, 1969, p. 86). Whatever is accomplished in this life pales into insignificance compared with the next. The Church is so special that one day God the Father will present her to Jesus as his Bride. Even creation itself waits in eager expectation for that day (Rom. 8:19). At that time, the greatest hallelujah chorus of all time will be sung, a glimpse of which is in Revelation 19:6–9:

> Then I heard what sounded like a great multitude, like the roar of rushing waters and like loud peals of thunder, shouting: 'Hallelujah! For our Lord God Almighty reigns. Let us rejoice and be glad and give him glory! For the wedding of the Lamb has come, and his bride has made herself ready. Fine linen, bright and clean, was given her to wear.' (Fine linen stands for the righteous acts of the saints.) Then the angel said to me, 'Write: "Blessed are those who are invited to the wedding supper of the Lamb!" ' And he added, "These are the true words of God."

Later in Revelation, St John describes the new Jerusalem (the Church), 'coming down out of heaven as a bride beautifully dressed for her husband' (Rev. 21:2). This leads to the consummation of the purposes of God – his dwelling will be with redeemed humanity for ever. Meanwhile, God's intent 'was that now, through the church, the manifold wisdom of God should be made known to the rulers and authorities in the heavenly realms, according to his eternal purpose which he accomplished in Christ Jesus our Lord' (Eph. 3:10–11) – in other words, as the heavenly powers (perhaps both demonic and angelic) observe the Church they see the inexorable unfolding of God's purposes, which must induce either fear or rejoicing. This wider vision of the Church should surely bring Christians to repentance for disunity and any other way in which we soil the garments of the Bride of Christ. 'Now to him who is able to do immeasurably more than all we ask or imagine, according to his power that is at work within us, to him be glory *in the church* and in Christ Jesus throughout all generations, for ever and ever! Amen (Eph. 3:20–1, italics ours).

Deeper understanding of contemporary prophecy

The gift of prophecy is one of the ministries which is manifested throughout the Church, whether or not branches of it recognise that fact or own the label 'charismatic' or 'Pentecostal'. Christians who have a vision of God's purposes for an aspect of his work, proclaim that vision and seek to bring it about by prayer, proclamation and action, are being prophetic. An obvious example in recent history would be the thousands of Christians in South Africa, who helped to bring about the demolition of apartheid. On a smaller scale, a leader or member of a local church may have vision as to the next step that church could take in, for example, mission projects. Clergy and ministers may be gifted in teaching, pastoral work or evangelism, but unless they either have the ministry of prophecy, or discover it in another leader, encouraging corporate discernment, prayer and action on that basis, the church is likely to lack any sense of direction. That is the ministry of prophecy in a nutshell (Eph. 4:11). By comparison, the gift of the word of prophecy (1 Cor. 12:10) is a message of encouragement or challenge delivered in a fellowship or worship context, of significance for that occasion. This may be given by the Holy Spirit to different people on various occasions. Both the ministry and the gift must be assessed by the church, especially to see that it is in keeping with Scripture.

An understanding of biblical prophecy may, in some circumstances, be important in assessing any contemporary ministry of prophecy which seeks to address major issues in the wider Church, or nation, or world. In 'charismatic' circles, many prophecies are widely circulated. Most are about a great revival coming to the UK, or Europe, or the entire Western world, or even the whole world. A smaller proportion are about terrible judgments, in the form of earthquakes, or financial collapse, or other dire predictions (usually with the proviso that these will be averted, given widespread repentance). Is either of these two main scenarios likely? The biblical balance in describing the Last Days (which, it should be remembered is a term covering all, or part of, the time between the first Pentecost and the Second Coming, or sometimes the end of that time) is between salvation and suffering, deliverance and persecution, victory and seeming defeat, glory and tribulation. Any prophecy which gives the impression of unmitigated triumph, without the cost of carrying the cross, is unbiblical, just as are those of doom and gloom, unrelieved by the possibility of transformation by the power of the resurrection.

In conclusion

In reviewing church history, the twentieth century has often been described as the Age of the Spirit. In a *primary* sense, that is a description of the entire church age, because the Church would not even exist without the operation of the Holy Spirit. There have also been many occasions when times of renewal and revival have swept sections of the Church down through the centuries. But in a *particular* sense, what is meant is the time when God gave major opportunities to the Church world-wide through the Pentecostal Churches (which were founded early in the century) and the Charismatic Movement (which began in the late 1950s) to rediscover something more of the vibrancy and spontaneity of the early Church. Christians were taught *how* to seek more of the gifts and power of the Holy Spirit, in addition to the better-known aspects of the Spirit's work (such as the fruit of holiness and his comfort and guidance). The outpouring of creativity which flowed from these movements resulted in transformation of corporate worship and involvement of a far higher proportion of church members in local and wider ministry. It has been estimated that a staggering third of all Christians world-wide belong to churches which would own a charismatic or Pentecostal 'label', and millions more have been influenced by some of the distinctive emphases of those movements. There is now a sense in which the Church is entering a post-renewal phase – not that those insights will be lost, but hopefully developed and matured. Sadly, there is a danger of looking for some new and exciting experience to cap the last particular wave of the Spirit, which could result in experience-centred rather than Christ-centred faith.

It is our prayer that, instead of falling further into that error, the Church will rediscover the wonder of biblical prophecy, so that the twenty-first century becomes the Age of the Coming King. No one can be certain whether Jesus will return in the new century, but every Christian could begin to pray for his coming, so that it becomes a major emphasis in the new millennium. Christian preachers and teachers could ensure that eschatology is given a prominent place as subject matter. We can all work to extend God's kingdom, so that as many as possible will bow the knee in loving reverence, rather than fear, when Jesus comes. We should all draw on the resources of the Holy Spirit, to help us to be disciples who will not be ashamed when he appears. Each local church and denomination could ask whether or not they bear any resemblance to the Bride of Christ, taking necessary steps of repentance and new beginnings. All Christians should pray and work for greater unity, so that the Body of Christ will not be so fractured when Jesus returns. And any readers who are enquiring about the Christian faith could pray now for forgiveness for the past; for Christ's gift of eternal life both now and beyond the grave; and for a willingness to love and serve the Coming King with all their heart, soul, mind and strength. One day, every eye will see him, and every tongue confess that he is the Sovereign Lord of heaven and earth. In fact, God will 'bring all things in heaven and on earth together under one head, even Christ' (Eph. 1:10).

In considering the vast purposes of God, what could be more encouraging than this biblical prayer (Jude 24–25):

To him who is able to keep you from falling and to present you before his glorious presence without fault and with great joy – to the only God our Saviour be glory, majesty, power and authority, through Jesus Christ our Lord, before all ages, now and for evermore! Amen.